Becoming
a Duchess in Red

Becoming
a Duchess in Red

by
Millie Lathan

WINGS
PUBLISHERS

Published by
Wings Publishers, LLC
P O Box 11530
Atlanta, GA 30355

Second Edition Text © 2014 by Millie Lathan

Editorial by Stacy Mattingly
Design and Layout by Nicola Simmonds Carmack
Cover and icon art, "Whorl" © Caroline Lathan-Stiefel

Quotation credits
"Beautiful Dreamer" Stephen C. Foster, 1864
"The Glory of the Garden" Rudyard Kipling, 1911
Lee Bailey, *Country Desserts,* Clarkson N. Potter, Inc, 1988
Charleston Receipts, Collected by Junior League of Charleston, South Carolina 1995

All rights reserved. No part of this publication may be reproduced, stored in a retrieval system, or transmitted in any form or by any means – electronic, mechanical, photocopy, recording, or any other – except for brief quotations in printed previews, without permission of the authors.

Manufactured in the United States of America

10 9 8 7 6 5 4 3 2 1
First Edition

ISBN 978-1-930897-22-9

To my grandchildren,
Bonnie, Robbie, Gray, Sam,
Charlotte, Louise, and Eli,
so they may know the family stories
that I love to tell.

Request vs. Bequest

Alas, a first edition—like the firstborn—is often incomplete, somewhat lacking in finesse, a little too repetitive, and at times inconsiderate. The second edition of our duchess's story is an attempt to rectify these issues. The criticisms have been heard and adjustments made. The author has been most grateful for all the advice.

One oversight was brought to the duchess's attention—with quite a poignant plea—by a dear friend who could not understand why "The Summer in Edinburgh" had been left out. "Wasn't it the best time you ever had? Did it not change your life forever? Is not Scotland—and the sound of bagpipes—the grandest memory from those college years?"

"Yes, yes, yes," the duchess affirmed. She tried to explain that dealing with a hundred years of family history did require a tremendous amount of editing. Doesn't the narrative flow have its own imperatives? Besides, Scottish metaphors are so worn and tattered, and who really cares about two privileged Southern girls setting off for their junior year experience, if only a summer, abroad? Nothing really happened in Scotland anyway....Just joy.

So, in response to the request, rather than an overly romanticized story that would never suit the sophisticated, twenty-first-century taste of you, the descendants, here is a list of what you might consider taking with you when you step out on your own for a journey of exploration, the pure pleasure and exhilaration of which will rarely be duplicated, no matter how short or long your life.

1. A lot of reading is a prerequisite.
2. You will need a traveling companion who has both imagination and the willingness to experience with relish even small things.
3. I suggest you bring a stylish, light-weight red coat. You will spend at least one night in it, so don't bring one that wrinkles too easily, as you want to look more than presentable the following day. And don't forget a pair of great sunglasses. You will probably lose them, but it won't matter when you do.

4. You will need a car in order both to get off the beaten path and to reach your destination, and even if you can't drive a stick shift, the rental agencies don't seem to care. You can also always join someone later who has a Humber Hawk, that is, if you do not mind simple picnics in the rain with only cheese and bread and a bottle of wine to pass around.

5. There should be one poet, really two—one dead and one alive.

6. A surprise kiss should be included, even if he is wearing a borrowed kilt. You cannot imagine what the addition of the kilt will do for the experience.

7. You should be willing to befriend a person a little older than yourself, otherwise you will never figure out how to get the train to Troon, see the British Open, and have tea with a young man who will become as famous as Jack Nicklaus became.

8. Do pack a small notebook: you may not have time to write much, but the few jottings you make may be your treasured bequest—certainly better than my list—for your grandchildren to enjoy.

9. On your return, you will need to refrain from: gushing on and on, calling or writing a letter, attempting to make scones, or wearing that burning hot Harris Tweed. But do run out and buy a bottle of bubbles, and blow a few to remind yourself that the joy you just experienced is now gone. You will never again capture the kind of delight you experienced so vividly, in Technicolor, being even more precious for its ephemeral fragility. The greatest time you ever had is but a bubble disappearing into space, not even leaving much of a story in its place.

The Story

There is always a beginning.

Once Georgia was a land of great beauty and contrasts, where tall pines boldly and cleanly reached for the skies and ancient live oaks majestically stood twisted and bent, burdened, it seemed, with gray moss and dark secrets. Swaying marshes, harboring the wild and the free, flowed uninterrupted to the sea, and worn fields with their red-clay scars stretched into the beyond. It was a land full of promise and failure, with a summer so bountiful your arms would ache and a winter so brown and barren only the foolish would stay. There the spring again pierced your heart, as only white lace and ruffles can do; and fall returned, ever golden, triumphant, polished in glory like the buckeye, stashed in a pocket now, for the luck it will bring.

The Queen and her first born

It was into this place that a princess was born. She was beautiful as all babies are beautiful, and her parents, the king and queen, were certain she would grow up to be both gentle and kind, yet strong and sure to rule one day with grace and wisdom. A war was raging, but it was far away on the other side of the world. The South had had her turn, and this was Georgia, after all: 1941. Still, the king did not realize there are many kinds of battles and defeats that always remain to be endured—until it was almost too late.

One cold December day, the king woke up to see the enemy's fires on the horizon. He quickly bundled his little princess and called to the queen. They gathered all their precious possessions and placed them in packs on their backs. They then filled an old brass chest with gold, silver, and what dreams they dared remember and buried it all before they left. The king was sure he could escape the battles raging within; survival was now the most important thing. Surely he—or his descendents—would reign here again one day.

And just as if the past had never been, the king and queen and their little princess left their grand station in life and moved—really just a short distance away—into a small house (though not too small): another county for sure. Their royal trappings were few, their only staff was Mattie, but all were alive and safe. The war soon ended, two more babies were born—another princess and a prince—and the family began anew.

No one suspected they had ever been royalty, much less that they planned to rule again, but the king and queen and their three children knew who they were. They knew about the buried chest, and they saw their magnificent kingdom, the fields and forests of Georgia, was still intact; they thought maybe, just maybe, one day it would all be theirs once more. Meanwhile, Mattie was there to play with the children, and the king was home every day to help out when needed. Yet the family also knew the enemy is always close—threats abound—so even the children kept small packs on their backs. This family was ready, if need be, to run and head for an exit again.

The King

Let's talk a little bit about the king. Our king loved his family, his not-so-little house, and the memory of his buried treasure chest. And to everyone's surprise he did not seem to miss being king at all. Well, why should he? He was still very handsome with a regal mustache, elite bearing, and a finely tailored tweed jacket. He was an experienced horseman, although he never rode, because he had broken both wrists in a riding accident (and thus did not need his horses, barns, nor all the bother of stables and attendants).

He was an excellent marksman, and though his large estate was only a dream from the past, he still had his prized dogs in kennels in the backyard and his fine guns ready in the closet if anyone were to invite him to shoot. He was an expert fisherman who tied his own flies, who only caught the most elusive fish in the clearest of mountain streams. Why own the stream when you have the knowledge of a talented guide? His guide was Crockett, and you could find no better fisherman, a man who even brewed his own homemade wine.

If the king needed to walk the walk of kings through a large, impressive ballroom, he had his gentlemen's club. If he longed to joust with young knights, he could watch over the high school football team. He still had exquisite taste, and if you were quiet and good, he might take a piece from his pack and tell you about the perfection of a Chinese bowl. And he had a full-time job training his little princesses and prince to be great rulers one day. He was a devoted teacher, a well-trained physician, and you felt very secure in his care.

Don't misunderstand me. This king was not perfect—no kings are—nor was he completely happy. He had left his kingdom and buried his fortune, and perhaps both the kingdom and the fortune never existed, but for sure he had wandered astray from his true station. Therefore, he had to be very careful with his money, a business that took a lot of his energy and concentration. He kept all the necessities for any merry-making tightly locked up from, he said, the staff. Everyone knew it was from the queen.

Being so careful with his money was a big job. He hated spending it. His pretense was that any expense was excessive, but there could have been other reasons. He was proud of his penury, but was he really a miser and even a little bit cruel? Don't forget all castles have dungeons; his was no exception. However, his greatest flaw (or, shall we say, the real tragedy of his life) was…he didn't understand the queen at all.

The King and protector

The Queen as a curly headed child

The Queen

The Queen was truly beautiful. Not beautiful in a silly, vapid sort of way, but in that unforgettable, mysterious, let-me-light-your-cigarette-and-dance-with-you way. And she did love to dance, to be sought after, to be chosen, and not just once—for had not the king chosen her above many others?—but over and over again.

She had a beauty intensified and brightened by her rare imagination. She could weave intriguing stories that drew you closer and make adorable dolls out of old socks and stray buttons that intrigued your fancy more than anything purchased in a store. And she could cook as only the truly inventive can. She would blend strange ingredients and have you waiting in anticipation, ready for a taste. Or she could take the most basic of things—butter and sugar, or even a grapefruit—and concoct a wondrous delight. Usually dishes came with some magical story from her past. Even her turnip greens and black-eyed peas had special powers. Eaten on New Year's Day, they guaranteed fame and riches.

You always wanted more of what she served. And she was also just great fun. Everyone agreed about that.

However, this queen (as queens often are) was just a little mad-crazy and very, very mad-angry. And the king simply could not get straight which mad she was, or when.

The mad-crazy part is frankly beyond my expertise, or anyone else's for that matter. The queen was nobody's fool, and she was not about to let any helpful wizard into her head. The wizard was certainly after her imagination and wit, and she was holding onto those with all her might. The closest anyone ever came to penetrating the maze was to suggest in a most professional way that relating to her was like relating to a dot-dash, dash-dot personality: on-off, off-on. For sure it kept the king confused.

The very, very mad-angry part is another story. Beautiful people are different from the rest of us in many ways. She knew

The young Queen

that others loved looking at her. She could see it in the way their eyes lit up and in how they would smile when they saw her. She appreciated how they would linger and come closer. Even the handsome Bobby Jones called her name and waved from across the East Lake putting green as he made his way towards her. If you too are beautiful, you may also have experienced this phenomenon, so you may also know you want more of it. The queen had enjoyed that divine spotlight, where everyone had drawn closer and lingered and smiled with lit-up eyes, and she wanted it back. She knew how much fun it had been to wave and hear the cheering. In actual fact, she had only ridden one float, as the Turkey Queen in Hapefille, Georgia. Still, she had heard those intoxicating cheers. She needed a crowd outside her house, waiting.

And, yes, she missed the "couture" clothes that might look so elegant on her. Who is going to know that you are queen if all you wear is a white blouse from Rich's? The king had his one fine jacket, but as a queen, she needed many, many dresses made of velvet and satin in magenta and cerise. She needed outfits you could let drop to the floor after you had worn them but once. (She often did just that—drop her clothes to the floor and step proudly out of them. The little princess was never quite sure if the queen expected Mattie to pick them up later or whether the queen was practicing what any queen would do if she were to come back late at night, exhausted from all the revelry.) She could be famous, sought after, even desired, if she only had some of those jewels buried who-knows-where. She was most certainly mad.

And the balls the king had promised her. Where were they? He knew she loved to dance—that she wanted her dance card full and to be chosen again and again, to move across the floor as if she were floating, to sing along with all the latest hits. Couldn't she design and orchestrate the best parties—with surprises tucked in the napkins, clever drinks both sublime and intoxicating, and live animals as centerpieces? A walk through the club's ballroom was not ever going to satisfy her. She wanted to dance and dance and dance with a big band playing. Of course she was angry.

And how did she feel about the not-too-small house, so far from diplomats and senators and other lords and ladies of the realm? It was not really the size or the location that enraged her so, but where were the craftsmen, the gardeners, the upholsterers, the oversized paintings, the staff? These were really what made a house a castle. Had the king not promised her all this when he asked for her hand?

You knew—even the children knew—how mad she was. When a lady walks out into her yard with her hair all frizzy from a too-tight permanent and lugs a mile of hose around from morning to night, day after day, in the hot Georgia sun, until she is wet all over with common sweat (and the too-tight permanent is definitely a disaster now), you know that the lady, the queen, is mad, really angry, about something.

Here, perhaps, you may interject, Why didn't she tell the king how she felt?

Darling (she might have said in a nice, playful voice), may I please have some new clothes?

Or, Come, honey, ask me to dance. Or this: My most honored king, just one gardener, just one.

Or even: Dammit, I need a drink and a new pocketbook.

Maybe she did say all those things in a sincere and sweet voice; maybe she said them many times over in a rather too strident tone. Maybe the king simply did not hear or did not have the money at the time. Maybe he was just a little cruel, or maybe he didn't give a damn (he had dated Margaret Mitchell before the queen). Who knows?

Conflicts and disasters just come, and certainly the king and queen knew that, but who would have thought the fires that had forced them to run would still be smoldering so boldly within their hearts? Whatever the reason, the beautiful queen often took to the bed in broad daylight and pulled the covers over her head.

The royal family

Or she would jump up early in the morning and begin the arduous task of watering the hydrangeas, and the very long lengths of hose would move slowly back and forth across the yard all day long. She would have a garden.

Why, you ask, did she not bundle up her children, fill her pack with a few little things, and run? Wasn't she the one who'd always said, "Find the exit first"?

Why, you ask, did the king not stop singing, "Beautiful dreamer / wake unto me," as if his beautiful wife was expected to dream herself out of her disappointment and madness?

These are important questions, but they are not for this story to unravel. The king and queen's twisting relationship is but a theme from the overture. The stage must be set. Let the princess's story now be told.

Meet The Princess

In the beginning, the little princess was an adorable child. She was bright, had light brown curls, and was adored by her father and mother, who spent hours telling her enchanting stories about their past. And then, as it always happens in fairy tales, the enchanting becomes enchanted, and the unimaginable unfolds. One event that set everything else in motion—or so thought the princess—was the birth of Princess Number Two, and then (before you could catch your breath), a Prince, no less, came forth. Princess Number Two was not just a beautiful baby—she was a knockout. With more blond curls than anyone deserved and commanding amber eyes, she was a relentless force who demanded everyone's attention from the minute she was born. The Bonnie Prince also had his own dashing set of curls, but if you are the last child and the first and only son, nothing else is needed.

Of course the king and queen started to look lovingly at these two newer babies and almost forgot about Princess Number One, the princess who by all rights would be queen one day and rule the realm. The real trigger, though, was not the birth of the siblings, nor the queen and king's loving attention to them, but the jealousy that was swelling inside Princess Number One's own heart. And because jealousy attracts the most terrible of witches and demons, our little princess began to grow in the strangest ways.

First, it was her feet: they grew and grew despite everything the princess tried to do to stop them. I do not mean grow in the sense that every child grows—when you get so excited that you're moving up the scale of life and acquiring new privileges and honor. No, I mean grow as in out of control so that no shoes anywhere fit. I mean grow (and do not think our little princess was unfamiliar with the story of Cinderella) as in way beyond the size that might fit into that glass slipper.

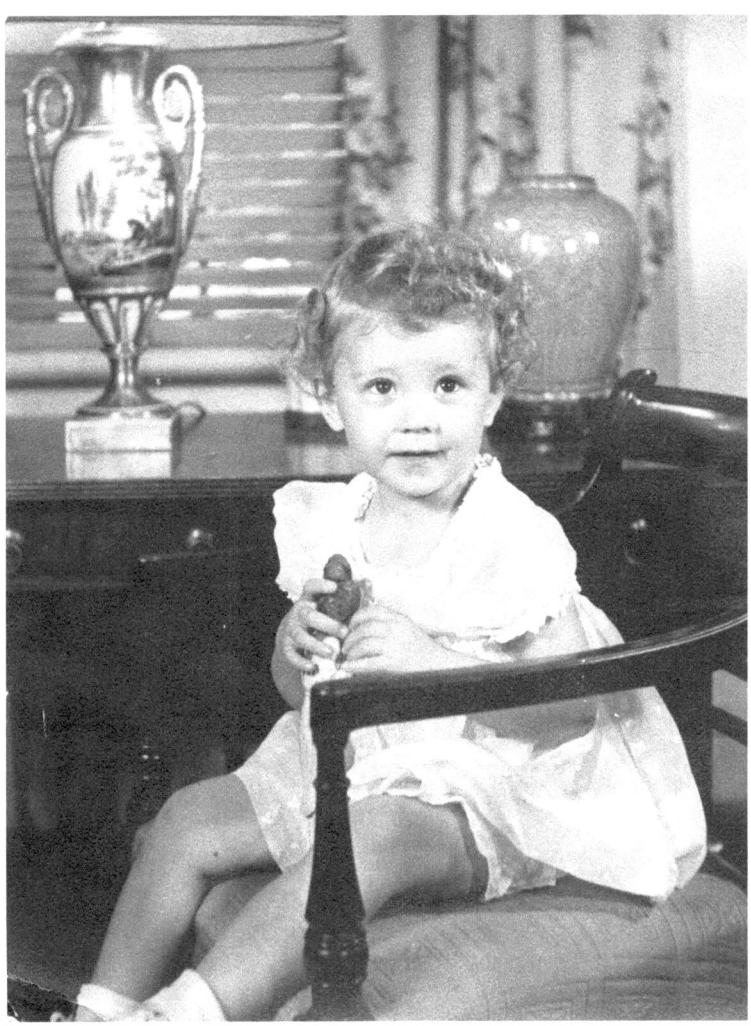

The Little Princess

Princess Number Two takes the reins

Not just the feet, but before you knew it, the nose started. And then the arms. This had to be the work of a witch. Where was her fairy godmother, anyway? Why didn't her neck grow so she would be a lovely swan, or her heart grow so she would love the poor, or her hair grow long and silky so that at least she could act the part of a princess in a play, or her breasts grow so she could hold up any strapless gown that might find its way to her closet? No. This was definitely the work of some cunning fiend, and it did exactly what it was probably designed to do: this growing curse only fueled the little princess's jealousy, and so the jealousy, like the feet and the nose and the arms, grew and began to pour out of the little princess through her cold, sweaty hands.

I could tell you the whole point of this story—and a thousand other stories for that matter—right now, and we could all go to sleep. But if I tell you the point directly, you will not hear it. That is just the way the human mind works. We seem to love stories, the stranger the better, and so we refuse to listen unless you tell us a story first. Pay close attention to what happens, and you may see what it is I am trying to tell you.

While our dear sweet princess was in a stew, dealing with untold body failures and uncontrolled jealousy, a horrible, worldwide plague descended upon the land and crept into every corner. No one had any idea where it came from, why it did the terrible things it did, or how to stop it. This tale takes place in the twentieth century, when scientists knew about bacteria, vaccines, and penicillin; but all the great scientists were baffled by polio—even the king had not a clue. It seemed to thrive in crowds, in summertime, and around swimming pools, but other than that, no one knew where it managed to hide or what encouraged it to flourish. It especially liked to inflict itself on children; the more innocent, the more likely they would be struck. And the ravages of the disease were devastating. Your limbs shriveled up, and you couldn't breathe, much less walk or run or play. The only hope you had was to be rolled into a huge, round iron machine that did your breathing for you, and then if you were lucky, after months and months, they let you out with all your limbs shrunken and twisted to walk if you could with the aid of awful, hollow, clanking braces. The news reels at every movie seemed to delight in showing you all this—the huge iron lungs, the banging restraints—accompanied by the deep, resounding voice of a newscaster, as if there was something you could do.

Our king was terrified: for the first time ever, it seemed, he was powerless. So he did the one thing everybody else did. He locked the children up.

This was the end of the princess, all right. She was locked up in her boiling-hot room (there was no air-conditioning in those days to speak of, and the king would've been too tight for such a luxury if there had been). There were no televisions, computers, iPhones, or video games. The princess was far too ugly now for any prince to come galloping to the rescue, and she was far too scared of being disfigured by this disease—even more than she'd already been by her own demons—to think about escaping herself.

Locked away like Rapunzel—when common folk might cry, "This is not fair, or shout, I give up"—a true princess takes it in stride. This is one skill royal blood possesses. Royalty's most valuable inheritance is not in some buried chest. No, their real crown is this talent to thrive under the most daunting of circumstances and to survive in really quite glorious, unexpected ways. Take special note. The task of survival is your responsibility, and if you are true royalty, you will survive regally. But I do suggest you start practicing now.

Our princess did just that. She had not failed to hear her father humming and singing, even playing, one of his few records (the aforementioned "Beautiful dreamer / wake unto me…"). And she bought it hook, line, and sinker (no sinker, of course, if you are a dry fly fisherman). She was like that speckled brown trout who

Just imagine

leapt high, its shimmering body arched miraculously in the air, its flashing silver tail powerful and strong, as it jumped from the safety of the shoals to reach for the deftly tied fly, and then fell back, still spinning into the net, caught. Yes, she was caught. She was caught by the sublime idea that you can imagine yourself out of anything.

The queen had turned up her nose at the notion, but the princess decided right then that she would be that beautiful dreamer. Now, forced to stay inside for those long naps, she had time to dream, and dream she did. Since there was no one to say otherwise, she could pretend to be as beautiful as anyone. Entranced by her shimmering dreams and shielded from odious comparisons with her very talented siblings—and avoiding the hitherto fore-observed absence of lingering looks from strangers—she found other benefits in being a captive.

First, she learned to read. Not by force, not by observing very strict rules—she learned to read by reading. She read and read, and the queen read and read to her children. They read fairy tales, nursery rhymes, comic books, cookbooks, the newspaper, historical novels, the Encyclopedia Britannica. Not the Bible, as I remember, but everything else printed that they could get their hands on. They read indiscriminately, every word, just for the pure joy of reading anything. It was a wonderful education in which there were no restrictions. Nothing was inferior or superior, too babyish or too complex. Every word was there to be had.

And then there was the fudge. When things were really dreary, the queen would find some hidden chocolate, sugar, and butter, and everyone would gather for the greatest show on earth. No stage set could come close to matching the wonder, the subtle magic, even the glamour of sugar turning into a shiny, creamy delight. And the danger of the very hot sugar only added to the drama. You could not get too close, only peek around, and you had to be quiet or she might mess up, and the exact moment that one must stop beating would be lost, and the whole thing would have to be thrown away.

So our little princess grew into an adolescent princess, well versed in dreaming, reading, and the art of the theatrical…yet forever captive, it seemed. Finally, the king let his children out when it was safe—at least safe enough. The princess walked to the bus stop (in those days there were no carriages, car pools, or chauffeurs set aside just for the children's ease and comfort), and she swore—not unlike Scarlett O'Hara, no rotten radish in her hand, but God was her witness—that she would never be locked up again.

Equipped with bus tokens, free to ride the Oglethorpe bus anywhere it could take her (mostly up and down Peachtree Road), and with many handkerchiefs in her backpack to mop up those sweating palms, the dreaming, reading princess was off to high school. And thank goodness the story does not end here, because high school for this princess was mainly a painful blur. I hope your experience is better. I hope, I hope.

High School

Oh, how it hurt. Oh, my goodness, the pain. First, there was the crippling pain of the shoes. Back in those days, in stylish, under-5-foot-4 Atlanta, there were no shoes—certainly not Papagallos—larger than size 8. No store could imagine anything larger, really, than a 7, and you were lucky if you found even one pair of size 8s; usually the only thing left was an odd green or purple. And if you haven't experienced wearing too-small shoes, let me tell you, it is absolutely the worst. It is all you can think about—how to hobble from one place to the next without dying. The princess began to quickly understand that she would never make it as a military leader, since she could not even stand this pain that no one, not another soul, seemed to have to bear. How would she withstand real torture by the Germans or the Russians when she could not even take a thin pair of shoes on her feet? Perhaps being queen might not be so great.

Then there was the even more excruciating pain of not being chosen. Why did anyone come up with the idea of Margaret Bryan's Dancing School, where the girls should line up on one side and the boys on the other, and after break-two-three, break-two-three, some boy, the love of your life, was supposed to see all your potential, intellect, and rhythm? You can be sure that not a single guy was able to see beyond the creamy, smooth necks of the laughing, budding beauties that Atlanta produced in great abundance, so our rather gangly princess had to stand there, alone, in horror.

And since one learns what one does, all the boys continued throughout all of high school down that single track, focused on the pursuit of fun and beauty. How could you blame them? It was hopeless, and the princess remained standing, unchosen.

To top it all off, there was the king, without his kingdom, now retired, always about, watching to make sure that his little princesses and prince were on their way to the top. The princess may have been better served if he had been a cobbler rather than a king with too much time on his hands.

Some very significant things did happen in high school, as they still do to this day. There was the time she saw Elvis live and in person. There was that Mardi Gras night when the princess first glimpsed the magic dust.

Mardi Gras

The wonder of being young is that you never question the impossibility of the task you are handed. This does make for many mistakes and embarrassing moments, but I urge you to never throw away this part of youth. Take it with you always. Never questioning the impossibility is how you make the impossible happen. And impossible will happen…just not always in the way you expected.

In the very early years of The Westminster Schools, there was a Mardi Gras tradition that each girl's class should build a float. Each class was given a theme, a minuscule budget, and an old wooden wagon. The floats would be judged, and the girl who rode the winning float would reign as Mardi Gras Queen. The intercom system, as this princess recalls, repeated: Elect a beautiful member of the class and Absolutely no parental guidance.

In their first year of competition, our princess's eighth-grade class was enthusiastic. They quickly elected the most beautiful girl among them, choosing Pocahontas as their heroine (actually, the only woman they really knew anything about), and they set to building a silken wigwam. They asked for no help from their parents and stuck to the budget.

It was a struggle from the beginning. It is very difficult to get a group of girls to work hard so that only one of them will win the prize as queen. Next, these girls' only experience in making anything was knitting squares for the poor in Africa (really, I think it was France with Mademoiselle's urging) and filling Red Cross boxes, which they had learned to fold themselves. The princess had spent hours making playhouses with Mattie, but they were of pine straw, and you had to imagine the walls and ceilings. Still, the girls worked on, fueled in large measure by the princess, who instinctively understood what winning was all about. Surely the eighth graders would at least beat the sophomores, who had chosen Joan of Arc as their heroine. After days and days, the sophomores had only a few sticks to show for their efforts, and those sticks had a long way to go.

On Mardi Gras Night, as the lights were dimmed, the eighth graders were still stuffing hymnals under the bamboo poles of the wigwam, which barely stood erect as the float lurched forward into the gym. Pocahontas in blue satin was truly lovely, but the eighth graders were as stunned as the sold-out crowd when the sophomores' float came into view. There was Joan of Arc, kneeling in prayer, her hands tied behind her, in a diaphanous white gown revealing her body and ethereal skin, a smoldering fire at her feet. Unbelievable! And hardly anyone was even Catholic.

Later that night, our princess stole over to the sophomores' winning float for a closer look. How had they pulled it off? First, she thought it was just the fire, or the idea of fire, that had thrilled the crowd, drawn them closer, held them, and stirred their imaginations. But there was no real fire. She saw the light fixture covered in red cellophane. Advanced technology, she thought; that's the secret. (She used a different word than technology, for in her mind, that word was only associated with Georgia Tech and football; but she did figure out that winning would require a lot of complicated equipment, far beyond her present grasp.) Still, technology wasn't the whole of it. It was the way it all came together—the way the red cellophane glowed and Joan of Arc's new beauty. Something had happened.

Then the princess looked closer. There on the float she saw a few specks sparkling. Those specks had bathed the creation into a glowing enchantment, while up close, the float was still only a pile of sticks.

She tried to sweep some of the shining dust into her backpack, getting more on her hands than in the pack. But now she knew that such a magic—whatever it was—existed. She realized that to win anything, to be anything (especially if you expected to be a beautiful queen one day), this was what was needed. She would go on to spend a lot of time trying to recapture that magical dust, to make it fall on her and around her, and to stand in its circle of light.

Knowledge of the dust is one thing, but trying to tell people about it, and conjuring it up for your own devices, is a very different matter. If anything, this new knowledge only brought more pain for our princess. Other folks simply did not get it, so her attempts at leadership fell flat—very flat.

And she never should have gotten it on her hands. She already was familiar with not being chosen, so she avoided all lining-up situations with a passion. It didn't take a genius to figure out that the only cover was to stay camouflaged and in the background. She knew that if she hoped to stay hidden, she would have to lie low when questions were asked to which only she knew the answers. But as if pulled by strange strings, her hands, it seemed, still covered in tiny specks (those hands that needed magic dust to stop sweating), had a mind of their own. They shot up in response to every question under the sun, every question in every class. And those hands waving wildly in the air sealed her fate, because she actually did know the answers. Or at least the teachers assumed so.

Other members of the class understood the trials of teenagers and that the body does things over which you have no control. But always knowing the right answer? That was unforgivable. The princess learned quickly that magic dust does not perform necessarily as one would want or in ways one can predict.

Why hadn't the dust transformed her, like it did Joan of Arc, into a beautiful heroine? Why didn't it make her hands behave? It is not easy being a princess with only your hands covered in magic dust. Yes, high school, even with its important moments, remained a painful experience.

There is one more terror, but at least it was shared by all the girls. Hair was big in the fifties. I know it got bigger in the seventies, but it was Very Important in 1956. One made huge sacrifices in one's attempts to get it right. Even the very beautiful, with their creamy skin and liquid eyes, had to make sacrifices. The key sacrifice was sleep. No one—not even the most perfect—could sleep in those metal rollers, held on by steel clips. The rollers and clips always found a particularly tender spot on the head, pressing into the skull with malice night after night. Still, this regimen was absolutely necessary for the hair to be just-so. No one complained about the hours it took to roll the hair on the rollers, which only got larger each year, or the extra time needed to undo them before school; no one questioned the necessity. Everyone believed it was the right thing to do, and so we did it, heedless of the pain, though desperate for a good night's sleep. Why do we continue to do such things—rolling up the hair every night only to spend hours combing it back down the next day—even when it obviously hurts so much and accomplishes nothing? Is common culture that powerful a force?

I guess it was the music that carried this generation through. You've seen the old movies where girls in wide, twirling skirts and boys with ducktails dance to the new rock-and-roll as they make plans—destined to fail—to escape into adulthood. This does not get close to what the princess and her group experienced during this decade. There was no angst for them. First of all, everyone felt safe. They probably were safe, safe in their ignorance, but also just safe, at least for that moment and in that time. After all, things were run by Presbyterians, who had everything planned well ahead.

Of course, there were rebels, but the rebels raced their cars on a stretch of Northside Drive that the drag racers' parents basically controlled. Most people rode their horses faster than they dared drive their cars. Who would want to dent one of those beautiful, swept-back fenders anyway, or scratch that radiant, pure finish? The only motorcycle belonged to one of the elite whose grandfather's excellent hand had penned Coca-Cola's famous logo. That grandson was not about to risk his life foolishly by driving too fast when he was idolized just for leading the parade.

It would be a few more years before anyone got pregnant (at least that people knew of). Everyone smoked, but no one had heard of pot. Some drank, but perhaps because so many parents drank to excess, the children were a little more careful. Maybe there were just too many Baptists. Drinking was simply not an option for the princess, as it was against the school rules and her father's rules, and she obeyed.

It was the music that truly intoxicated everyone anyway. It was the music you could not get enough of. It was the music that told tales, moved you, transported you. Music was everyone's secret society. That was what separated you from your parents and united everyone born in 1941. Music was the exotic, sexual expert. It was forever new and young. There they were, leaning over the record player, listening carefully to "Work with Me, Annie." by Hank Ballard and the Midnighters. Some knowing soul would explain what the words meant. And then all would jump up to practice the steps over and over again.

The newness became an addiction. Not just the lyrics were new, but also every rhythm, every beat, every sound—all for the first time heard. New songs came on the radio almost every day, and a new, moving beat exploded into your life. Everyone had to stay glued together so as not to miss the next breaking hit. The excitement was palpable. Everyone, including the princess, felt as if they were at the center of the universe. They were living in a moment when everything important was about to happen; looking back, this generation was truly at the epicenter.

The blinking population marquee at the Darlington Apartments may have reminded all that Atlanta was a small town, but these war babies were soon to ride the revolutionary waves of the twentieth century, and they were not afraid. Our adolescent princess was not afraid, either, because in spite of her secret pain, in spite of never being chosen, in spite of the many body woes, she was there in the midst of the great revolutions of all time, supported by this wonderful rock-and-roll music. Her world was turning upside down, yet she was safe, probably as safe as she or any other princess would ever be again; free as long as the Oglethorpe bus opened its doors; and still dreaming wonderful, shimmering dreams, sprinkled with the possibility of a transformative, magical dust that both caught the light and added mystery and beauty in a single pass.

The Quest For The Kingdom

The princess was not the only one trying to recover the magic dust. The king himself had been quietly busy, planning his own campaign to recapture lost territory. The family needed its kingdom back, if only for a few weeks. The queen had had it, burning up in her un-airconditioned house all those summers, locked up in perpetuity with her saggy-baggy diaper-pants brood. No adventures. No parties. Day after day, the same. So the king, with a very small budget, no army to speak of, zero support from any constituency, and only poor secret intelligence, started looking for a place where they might experience the magic, even if just for a few days.

    His first foray was to the coast: the white sand beaches of northeastern Florida. He was forced to bypass the much better choice of Sea Island due to financial constraints, but he was sure that if the family never saw Sea Island, they would find all the sun and sand they needed at Atlantic Beach. That first excursion was a total failure. The car trip, made at only forty-five miles an hour so as to save money on gas, lasted forever. On the way down, they had to smuggle Mattie into the motel after dark. (Do not forget: This was the late 1940s. Segregation was the standard, and it would take the entire Kennedy clan to end the practice in hotels and motels throughout our country almost twenty years later.)

Car with royal bounty

Though no one said a word then, everyone knew that this was wrong. Many years later, the queen did try in some way to rectify the situation when she took Mattie and her mother on a trip to Paris. That night the family simply got no sleep. Whatever the real reason, no one raved about the beach; none liked the sand in their toes nor, as it was off-season, the freezing ocean.

On his next try, the king shifted closer to home, reasoning, "We're Georgians, not Floridians." Maybe the family needed to go somewhere more like camp, where the children could learn new skills and the king and queen could fish. We don't need to dwell on what a disaster that fish camp experience was, but it did probably hold the world's record for the most concise vacation ever taken by

Fishing in Maine

a family of five. In Georgia, heading a short distance south of Atlanta means, "Sorry, still in the gnat zone." The queen refused to get out of the car. No Georgia long-leaf-pine picnic for her.

    One had to hand it to the king. He did keep on trying, and he was listening to what the queen was saying. Their next attempt—to the Alabama coast—he was sure would be perfect. The children were bewitched by the Spanish moss. Everyone loved fried shrimp, especially the queen. Their destination was a garden—even better, a garden made possible by Coca-Cola. And it was a wonderful trip. The Bellingrath Gardens were beautiful, the air fragrant, and both the king and queen were inspired to try camellias in their own backyard.

But poor king. The trip home, again, was way too long, way too hot, and the car too crowded. When the turnip greens he bought at the open market in Union Point exploded out of the pressure cooker and all over the kitchen (he'd insisted they had to be cooked that night; the queen was furious, exhausted, and just might have sabotaged the whole thing), it was plain there would be no more trips to the lovely seaport city of Mobile and its environs.

I've told you, have I not, that royalty does not give up? They know the real thing when they see it, because they have experienced it. They are royalty. So our king trudged on. You have to admire his tenacity. The family continued on the quest, not just for a nice vacation spot, as everyone else in their right mind was doing, but for that magical kingdom they once possessed—even if it was but for a week in August.

The king became more focused and organized. He spread out maps, studied brochures, called in advisers; mainly, he listened to his own heart and to that of his queen. This quest became his life's work.

You have been forewarned that magic dust does not behave in totally predictable ways. One man's vision of paradise might well be another man's primitive fish camp. It all depends on the vagaries of that elusive, falling dust, but the High Hampton Inn in North Carolina was, for this family, the dream come true. The Grimm Brothers could not have imagined a more magical fantasy.

First and foremost, the mountains of North Carolina were only a short distance away. One stop for breakfast and you were there. Fighting was reduced instantly by fifty percent.

Secondly, and probably more importantly, the mountains were cool. The family could actually feel the temperature drop as the twisting road climbed up. This coolness was more than just a

The big catch

feeling on the skin. Coolness meant large blazing fireplaces, even in the summer, and smoke rising in a blue haze from stone chimneys. Coolness meant cashmere for the queen, that soft, cozy cashmere, which transforms even an ordinary outfit into something elegant. Coolness invited you to go on a long hike or put on riding boots for a trail ride. Coolness meant hot tea in the afternoon and a good book, maybe on the porch but even more likely inside next to that roaring fire so carefully laid by woodsmen in plaid coats. Coolness was a fresh blast of mountain-scented air as you stepped down onto boulders alongside a clear, rushing stream. Coolness was a luxury that Southern royalty relished and adored.

And it was so green—all manner of green. Not just the bright green of new leaves, but every known shade of green: the soft green of manicured fairways, the dark green of Carolina hemlocks, the gray green of the white pines, the true green of forest mosses, the shaped green of the boxwood hedges, even the red green of Halsted's famous beech.

In truth, the castle was really a lodge, but it was big and sat proudly on a hill. The driveway was long and twisting, your arrival slow and orchestrated. Staff leapt to welcome you back after your winter away. Mountain women sold bundles of galax leaves, which ensured that the wonderful scent of the mountains followed you into your room. I could go on, but suffice it to say, all of the family (even the queen) agreed that at last, if only for a few days in August, they were finally back, here in their proper, royal place. At last for all of them, the magic dust fell on High Hampton Inn.

The summer after her junior year, the princess was an exchange student to Greece. Though she hated missing even a single summer in the mountains, she was off to an adventure that was hers alone. This summer is a long story with many details and one of the most wonderful gifts the princess would probably ever receive. However, this was also the summer, when she turned her head away for one minute, that Princess Number Two grabbed the prince of all princes in—where else but?—the mountains of North Carolina, changing everything. Unfortunately, we have to leave the many adventures of July 1958. If there is time, maybe I will tell you more, but for now we must get our princess off to college. She was ready, at last, to get to the living part of her life.

"Hold That Tiger"

For this family, life seemed to be making a turn for the better. The king was satisfied that in the mountains he now had a kingdom he could call his own—though they only rented and just for a week. The king was also thrilled that his well-trained princess, with honors from high school, would be heading off to Boston. Even the queen paid attention to the princess and read all the magazines with her; together they loaded a huge trunk with worlds of skirts and suits, pocketbooks that matched, and monogrammed sweaters.

The princess was at last on center stage. One crisp September day, the whole family rose at three o'clock in the morning to properly escort the princess to the Atlanta airport (only a collection of World War II-era huts at the time) where she would take one (the cheapest) of the two flights to Boston. It felt like a coronation. It felt grand.

The princess had never seen the school and did not know a single person there, but she was excited beyond imagination. She was very prepared for everything—except for what happened.

In 1959, most people she met at her college had never heard of Atlanta, Georgia, and certainly had never been there. Some may have read *Gone the Wind*, but the setting was only imaginary, they thought. Few at Wellesley had even laid eyes on a Southern person of any sort. One began instantly to question why these people were so smart if they didn't know how great (or where) Sea Island was and showed no interest in fried chicken secrets. The princess had been warned they didn't eat grits, but she was shocked to learn they didn't even care that they had never tasted them.

In Boston, no one dared mention the word religion. In Georgia, everyone always asked right away where you went to church and always had something nice to say about each religion, whether you were Catholic (you lived in a big house and had lots of brothers and sisters) or Presbyterian (you did everything by the book and were always president) or Methodist (you had the second-best Sunday-night league and the very best hymns) or Baptist (you had the best Sunday league with the most popular boys) or Episcopalian (you had the one true religion). You could marry a Presbyterian, Methodist, and of course an Episcopalian. That sums up about all the princess knew on the subject of religion. Not much by your standards now. She knew nothing about being Jewish, except that you wore beautiful clothes; she had never seen a Muslim; and Hinduism and Buddhism for her evoked only bright colors and exotic idols per *The National Georgraphic*, surely not a viable faith.

At home, differences—insofar as they were conceived—were discussed, meaning everyone knew from the very beginning where everyone else stood. One considered oneself liberal because nothing was hidden; there were no clandestine gatherings. This is just the way it was. But in Boston, as noted, no one said a word. Even in biblical history class, one's personal religion was not mentioned. When you go to a new school, I suggest you find out beforehand what can and cannot be said, which topics are safe and which are not. Even though you are so well informed now, you may be surprised by your own ignorance as to what actually moves people to silence.

Also, the princess noticed that many classmates seemed afraid of something. They worried about which classes to take, where the professors had studied, were they in the right dorm with the most intellectuals, would anyone find out their grades, should they go into politics, etc. They wouldn't dream of getting on the MTA and riding into Boston just to see what was there.

Yet the thing they should have been afraid of, the thing that became apparent to the princess, was that a great many of these brilliant classmates (though, of course, Nora Ephron and Ali MacGraw would light up any room they entered) were just a little dowdy looking, a little too wholesome, and the thing they should have been worrying about they clearly chose to ignore. They should have been worrying about what they were wearing. Or a better lipstick choice. Definitely they needed radical hair do-overs. Instead, it seemed all anyone wanted the future to bring was the equal opportunity to wear an old sweater while freezing to death on a deserted island in Maine or to work as an assistant's assistant for a New York magazine. Few imagined going home to reign.

All this was an unexpected turn of affairs for our newly arrived princess. In Atlanta, everything was the opposite. If you were beautiful, you flaunted it. If you had brains, you hid it. If you were not beautiful, you relentlessly studied ways to mask your misfortune. You planned to rule one day, but you were taught from the beginning that this was a complex endeavor and that "au naturel" was but one of many disguises needed, certainly not a way of life. And what were all these women going to talk about if religion and glamour were off limits? The news? A better world? But, then, our princess was only a freshman.

In spite of being the outsider from the unknown region of the South, the little princess did thrive in this different environment and, in spite of herself, was radically changed by the experience. She was ready. She had been perfectly tutored by both the king and queen and all her female teachers. She had read and read. After those years of isolation and the pain of not being chosen, she was thrilled to jump into anything, and her thirst made her fearless. College did not disappoint. She had many phone messages to return; new friends reached out; she had a trunk full of clothes for any event (though nothing resembling a warm coat); the classes were all exciting and the library jammed with books. She learned about the fun of sitting at a round table for dinner and just laughing with these new, very witty companions.

She went to real museums and rode the subway in New York City. There were those unexpected moments when magic dust fell out of the sky and the whole world lit up. She exited a train at Hamilton late one night with only a full moon's reflection to light

Magic dust for the King and Princess

the way as she tramped through waist-high drifts to meet some unknown date for the weekend. She inhaled the scent of lilac, infused with the chill of a New England spring, as she walked awkwardly beside a Harvard freshman—just as young and as much a novice as herself. She told a story over and over about dropping quarters at the New Jersey tollbooth (there was no such thing as a tollbooth in Atlanta) and holding up lines of traffic as everyone spilled out of the rental car looking for the lost coins. They were headed to Princeton to meet the sons of corporate America, and they laughed even harder on the way home at how ridiculous their expectations had been.

In class, the princess saw strange poems shredded to pieces by an erudite professor's insights and then ignited with grandeur as he put them back together again. She sat in wonder as a painting was turned upside down with questions and suppositions only to be reloaded with meaning as the power of intention was released. She learned to strip away hundreds of years of decay from a New Testament parable in order to see a new, brighter clarity beneath.

Yet despite flourishing, she never felt fully at home, and she didn't understand until much later what her send-off, her coronation in the middle of the night, had actually meant. She thought those moments of incredible loneliness—when the New England dusk briefly shed its alien light (so different from the fullness of the Southern afternoon sun); when no one seemed to have any idea who she was, much less really care; when she realized that reading, even a very careful reading of sacred dogma, would never make her whole; when the many callers only temporarily lifted her heart—she thought those moments were nothing but homesickness. Faulkner must have been right, that there are ghosts from a Southerner's past, pulling one back to the land where one was born.

Perhaps she didn't understand—because who would at such a young age?—that her departure from home was not a coronation but an exile. She was in the midst of becoming one of those terrible footnotes—a person most everyone failed to notice. She was a discard, the three of clubs, buried in the deck, remembered as a statistic, a number, but never again needed to complete the royal flush.

Certainly she had heard the story often enough; the queen loved to chant it: "You always throw away the first pancake." It takes time for the iron skillet to reach the right temperature. The first pancake is there to soak up the extra fat. It is always too burned around the edges and too raw in the middle to be enjoyed. It is meant to be thrown away. "Flip it, like this, into the garbage."

The princess mistook this instruction for more of the queen's expert culinary advice. She never dreamed the queen meant her, even though the princess's trunk had been packed for a lifetime. Even though her return-trip ticket was never in the budget, except for Christmas and a summer holiday, and even then, reluctantly. Even though she received no letters from home, only care packages, which seemed to say, "You are there for a longer stay." She was just too scorched around the edges, too raw inside, to do. Yes, she was the first born, but that didn't mean she would be the one to rule. Sorry, my dear. There was a much abler, more beautiful Princess Number Two waiting for the crown, and a precious little Bonnie Prince not far behind. But our princess, the discard, the scrap, only felt a strange sadness. She never knew exactly why.

Granted, the sorrow never got the princess down for long. She did have energy. She loved Boston. She loved her many funny friends. She believed she would return home as a princess revealed after all. So she did everything a princess is expected to do. She drank tea with the house-mother. She had dates with the Wilson Sporting Goods grandson. She studied Joyce's Ulysses and valued every friendship from that class. She traveled to New York City to see plays and eat at famous restaurants with a Southern gentleman. She saw the Cape from a modernist poet's point of view. She shook hands with Teddy Kennedy and Lyndon B. Johnson. She learned on a weekend at Dartmouth that a Vietnam War was coming soon. She listened to Joan Baez ballads at Eliot House. She combed the stacks for old New Yorker magazines, looking for uncollected Salinger stories. She waited for the next James Bond thriller. She took the queen's birdbath to the White House. She never joined a sit-in, but she conspired to hear Martin Luther

King, Jr. preach at Atlanta's Ebenezer Baptist Church. She volunteered as one of the first tutors for Head Start, and she played the carillon with a black fellow student. She heard Paul Tillich in person, although she didn't understand a word he said. She knew little about sex, but she did find a suitable prince-in-waiting, handsome and strong, an Olympian who loved her and made her laugh.

And yet, it was not enough, you see, for no one from Atlanta was paying very much attention. First, in the short amount of time since the discarded princess had left home and graduated from Wellesley and then Harvard, the whole world had changed. Think: the sixties. You make long lists in your history and social studies classes of everything that transpired during that decade, but your family was living it; and it took everything everybody had just to hold on. People in Atlanta were very busy. Then, of course, Princess Number Two was a showstopper. She was talented, beautiful, and smart with large tiger-eyes that would never dim under the weight of a crown. And so, crowned she was, the Tiger-Eyed Princess, and it was a most festive occasion. At least from what the princess heard, for there was no ticket for her to attend.

But lastly, and very sadly for our wannabe princess, the king died after a very brief illness. From the beginning, the king had been old. He had retired long before the other, more powerful fathers. You knew he could die. He'd had gray hair for as long as the princess could remember, and his constant presence was a lot for a vulnerable adolescent to handle. No one needed the queen's reminders of how much older he was than she—twenty whole years.

THE QUEST

Lifted by the King

No Good-Bye

The king had always been there for the princess—cheering at every triumph, behind the scenes making absolutely sure everything would turn out perfectly for his little daughter. He was the one who told inspiring stories of an Indian princess named Red Feather. He was the one who drove her to countless tennis lessons and to horseback riding. He tried to find a cure for her many fears, got her the latest bestseller, bought the family piano, made and kept the dermatologist appointments, even took the princess to church, though he would not consider going inside himself. (He had sworn to everyone: Never Again.)

It was humiliating, though strangely comforting, to see a father so determined to get a child off the bench and onto a team—after all, she was tall and had those very long arms—that he would shoot baskets by himself day after day, hoping to lure her out to practice.

"Keep your eye on the ball" was his ever-repeating mantra.

Most unbelievable, he even hired some high school hotshots from another part of town as her coaches, thinking that maybe sex would be a carrot to get her excited and practicing. In spite of the evidence, he always believed she would excel as an athlete. He never acknowledged defeat. He believed in her, and he infused the little princess with his hopes. "Just keep your eye on the ball…"

Remember the matchbooks? No one knew how it started or why, but somehow the king got the princess interested in matchbook covers. In those days, cigarette smoking was at the center of everyone's life. Everywhere you went, matchbook covers were out in a bowl: sleek vehicles of salesmanship, elegant and smart, often gold-embossed and exotic. And if you but looked most anywhere, you could find a discarded one, thrown out or lost, partially spent or brand new, a neatly packaged reminder of a special place or divine experience. The king and the princess started picking up these stray mementos, turning them over and commenting on where they were from, guessing who lost them and when. For the father and his child, they became wonderful treasures and even great promises of adventure, just lying there on the sidewalk for any watchful person to discover. Thus, every new place you happened to go, even somewhere as boring as the dry cleaners, might be a source for some never-before-seen cover of delight.

The hunt turned into something quite different as the king began to enjoy seeing the princess find the covers. There were not that many restaurants in post-war Atlanta—really, only about four—and the king was in bed before most bars opened (there was only one nightclub, and it was a stretch to call the Dinkler that). The city was still in the Dry South. The king had to find other ways to preserve the thrill of the hunt.

Dapper days

He started calling on his better-traveled lord-and-lady friends, asking for their matchbooks, and he began to salt the walks. He would amble back and forth across the golf course, stealthily dropping covers for his child to find. And of course, she did find them and came to believe there was a treasure waiting for you if you would only look. When she finally saw through the ruse, she only gave a joyous laugh, for now she believed in the possibility of untold wonders and knew for sure that the king always had her back and would guarantee a find.

The king also shared uplifting stories of fortitude and endurance. Though he'd had but a nickel for breakfast at Columbia University College of Physicians and Surgeons, he was smart enough to choose between an apple or oatmeal each day;

Come Home for the King

and even though others laughed at his accent and he was forever hungry, he was still Omicron Delta Kappa and figured out how to get himself invited to the finest debutante balls and land summer tutoring jobs with the elite. "Your brains are not in your feet," he often said, but the little princess never quite understood what that meant, thinking perhaps she would be better off if they were.

 The only restaurant they ever visited other than the club (why eat out when your mother is such a good cook?) was the S&W Cafeteria. Every trip down the line began the same way. "Here is a quarter," the king would say, taking one out of his pocket. "It goes to the one with the smallest bill." The princess had no chance of winning, as the desserts were always first—shortcake piled high with fake whipped cream and strange-colored strawberries—and she loved the fried chicken. But she would try for the quarter anyway. While the younger siblings smirked at their victories, she thought, just wait till you're starving from all the training and see if you can resist. Just wait, she thought, as she set a large piece of coconut cake on her tray.

 Later, it was the king who fully understood her homesickness, as he too had been banished to the North for medical school in New York and for surgical fellowships to follow. It was the king who sent the princess ice skates in one package (the frozen pond, edged in ice-covered balustrades and topiaries can be yours) and southern greenery in the next, reminding her that Georgia would always be her home. Aside: When she opened that second box, the pine and magnolia perfume filled her sparse dorm room; and her Massachusetts roommate, who lived but a few miles away, wept with homesickness with her.

 When your father is a king controlling almost your every step, it is very hard to imagine him gone. So it was amazing to our discarded princess how quiet her experience of his loss seemed to be. Maybe because when she heard the news, she was surrounded by snow. It was her junior year. She was in New Hampshire on her first ski weekend. "Come home. Your father is dying." She cried all the way back, missing him already, but also a little fearful of how the queen, her mother, would react.

Unexpectedly, the king's death seemed at first as uncomplicated as attaching a stamp to a thank-you note or turning the page in a book. It flowed into time seamlessly. One moment, you are alive, and the next you have slipped out without a word. How could someone so powerful vanish just like that? The princess didn't even get to say good-bye.

As it turned out, she had nothing to fear from the queen. The queen focused on but one thing—her own newfound freedom. How could she, a queen enthroned, possibly deal with our princess's jealousy, sadness, empty future, or the injustice of it all, when she was about to begin her life again? In the end, after college and graduate school, our princess did return to Atlanta (believing that homesickness was her only problem), very well educated, with little fanfare, with no king to keep her safe, and sans the suitable prince she had commandeered, who, after but one visit to the High Hampton Inn, realized her kingdom was not for him… if it even existed at all.

The Treasure Map

Let's catch our breath for a moment, sit down, and take a look inside our princess's backpack. A new chapter in her life is about to unfold, and we need to see if she is truly prepared. Can you imagine what, at this point in her life, she has put inside her pack—what might be those most treasured artifacts to savor on life's journey or, at least, some of the very essentials, lest she need to make a fast exit?

You are right: there was a little magic dust still lurking in the stitching; not enough to transform many moments, yet it was there as a reminder that magic dust exists and that it can work miracles. In abundance were wads of crumpled handkerchiefs, eternal monuments to the reality of evil fiends and her own uncontrolled jealousy. But those handkerchiefs had come in handy on many occasions, and she was not about to abandon them. There was really very little else. Oh, yes, she also had one-third of the map to the king's hidden treasure trove. I forgot to tell you about that.

Frankly, I began this story hoping I could somehow leave this part out.

It is so hard to talk about money, social class, and inheritance. In America, supposedly, none of that is important. Yet in spite of the pitfalls ahead, we shall attack the problem head on. Money, money. Can even a song take away its very sharp edges?

In the South in the forties, there was very little money, and there were many, many stories about being poor. War, for one, had made things difficult. There was that war during which Sherman not only stole your chickens and cows, but even shot your dog. There was World War II, when every able-bodied wage earner was marched off to fight; even if you did have some money then, you could only get what your ration book would allow—a little sugar and margarine, into which you squeezed insipid yellow dye. There was then the The Great Depression, along with other little depressions and crop failures, wiping everyone out and fusing Southern culture into one giant, shared bowl of turnip greens and corn bread. The stories about the horrors of poverty multiplied, and every person had a tale of desolation and sacrifice. Even the relatively rich had stories to tell.

Such a stage was the only stage on which our dear king, now dead, had been given a part to play. Being so many years older than the queen, he had heard, on a daily basis and in real time, stories about how his family's fortunes and promising futures had been upended by marauding Yankees and collapsed financial institutions. He himself had lived through terrible poverty—even more terrible if you're the son of a Methodist minister and have to accept being poor as God's gift to you. And while, because of his age, he escaped the trip to the blue Pacific, he experienced what it was like to see every economic effort focused on the war, never on anything as mundane as a medical practice. Yet the king was sure he had figured it all out. How to be rich, that is. It was simple. He would bury his treasure—all one-thousand dollars' worth of Coca-Cola stock—and with time and patience, a fortune would emerge.

For now, he just pretended to be rich. He took the little princess by the hand, and every month they went downtown and parked the car in the bank's garage, as did the privileged class. He would explain how the stock market worked and how Mr. Glenn, a Methodist minister's son himself and now one of the richest people in Georgia, had convinced him that Coca-Cola was the one and only stock to own, where the treasure was to be hidden, how big it would grow, and how important it was never to touch your principal, no matter what.

As the children grew in age and the king grew more impatient with the queen, he told the little princess, "Do not fear. Your mother is crazy. But the money is safe because I have left it to all of you and your children. She'll never get her hands on it." He carefully composed his will, leaving the principal to his grandchildren—of which, at the moment, there were none—and the income from the estate to his wife and children, with a percentage of the income shared with his two sisters. At the sisters' death, or if the queen remarried, the income would be divided between the three children, leaving the queen with but a pittance. The bank would manage everything until the last of his children was deceased.

Was this will a good financial plan?

Absolutely not, if you are the queen. Hadn't she done her part, stayed locked up, with not even a drink, so that now, at last, she could live her life? She was ready to spend, and she needed the money.

Certainly not, said the administrators. If the king had had an ounce of kindness in his body, how could he have left his wife with only the income (which she must split) and without even a roof over her head?

Definitely not, according to the financial advisors. If you want long-term growth, you must diversify or expect to be wiped out.

Even the foolish queried, Why would a person give half his hard-earned estate to the government, whom he hated? It made no sense to anyone, except to the little princess, whose mind had been tampered with by the king.

There is nothing particularly noble about being poor. Both the queen and the king agreed, having experienced it first hand, that lack of money creates mostly pain. Access to capital is a necessity if anyone is to get ahead. A plan of some kind was needed. But this plan? Revolutionaries think they have the answer, but they come and go as the seasons. Economic theories are just that—mere theories. What is the one true thing about money that we must learn before we, like so many before us, make horrible mistakes in earning it, keeping it, ignoring it, wasting it, risking it, starting wars over it, or giving it to those we love? The one true thing is this: you will need it. That, my little ones, is guaranteed. And no handout nor inheritance, no matter how mercifully given, in spite of how thoughtfully and fairly administered—even if both houses of Congress are in complete accord—will suffice. You will need your own money, no matter your station in life. Get busy, go to work, and start saving. You will also need a plan of your own. Any plan will require time. Thus, you will need others to help carry it out. In our story, it would be the queen, the last person on earth you would've thought, who would make the king's terrible plan succeed.

The Map And The Queen

While death itself may be a silent experience, for those left behind, the aftermath is most often anything but a peaceful repose. I guess that's why the cinematographer uses bombs and machine-gun fire to express death, confusing death with its screeching aftermath.

All those who knew the king—friends, neighbors, especially family—were holding their breath. What fireworks would erupt when the queen discovered that she had been all but disinherited and, in spite of her freedom, was still bound by the king's old chains?

Perhaps they'd failed to remember she was royalty. I've already told you how those of royal blood do not take seeming defeat in expected ways. The queen did let out one appropriate sob, but oddly, there was no grand-scale visual display, no dramatic entrance or exit as the poor widow betrayed. She did not discuss any strategy. There was no hint of a felt unfairness, except a few asides to the princess, whom the queen considered a spy. Still, within a very short time, you knew she was up to something.

First, there were the many trips to the bank. The queen was rising early these days, giving herself plenty of time to dress—to get the lipstick right and the nylons on without runs. And in three short visits, she had secured the house in her name. Next she proceeded to move the now rather large magnolia trees she had so dutifully watered into different locations around the not-so-little house's yard. She had been studying perspective, it seems, and could now enlarge the appearance of the house with only a little help from a bulldozer and Atlanta's top landscape designer. How nice everything looked, and it cost practically nothing.

Next, she would have to get the children out of the house and off the payroll—certainly the girls. In other words, married right away.

Marrying off the Tiger-Eyed Princess, who had risen to the number-one position, was of course very easy. The only real problem with the fantastic prince the Tiger-Eyed Princess had come up with was that the queen was considering him for herself. After all, the crowned Tiger-Eyed Princess was only sixteen, while her intended was ten years older, very tall, very handsome, a great dancer with many connections, a trumpet player, and a man with the habit of wearing polka-dot handkerchiefs. This was a hard call. Somehow, the Tiger-Eyed Princess held her ground, and wedding bells did ring for her.

Marrying off the discarded princess was going to be much harder, meaning the rush was on. The queen kept the fires burning in the fireplace, homemade peach ice cream on the porch, music on the stereo, and she purchased a very long sofa for the living room (the queen was looking for tall and handsome in her future sons-in-law, and a make-out sofa should certainly fit). As luck would have it, a prince appeared without a too embarrassing delay. Later, the princess noted the irony when, after asking her spouse why he proposed, he answered, "You know, your mother was so attractive and friendly. It seemed the thing to do."

Now the final puzzle: with two daughters taken care of, what in the world was the queen going to do with a young, barely adolescent son?

The last born, the Bonnie Prince, may have been the youngest, but he was far from the least. If you are looking for a gold cord to hang onto, it is his story you should follow to the end. However, at the moment, he was only twelve, and the queen was desperate to focus at last on her own future.

Luckily, when it came to her son, she really had to do very little. Bonnie Prince was perfect and took care of the details of his growing up quite well by himself. Bonnie Prince always made good grades and was well liked and handsome. It is no wonder that both the king and the queen agreed totally on everything concerning him (he was the only thing they did agree on outside of Coca-Cola). He too was submitted to all the rigorous training that had so tormented both his older sisters, but his training seemed natural and expected. (It might be added that the king and queen had faced much resistance trying to perfect their first- and second-born children, but for some reason, the prince followed the program without a word of disrespect.) When he was plopped atop the horse at High Hampton, he neither cried out in fear like the discarded one nor charged the fences like Miss Tiger-Eyed.

Oh, Happy Day

He simply sat there proudly. When the king yelled, "Talk bass to him, Bubba" (the steed apparently not budging, only nibbling), the prince just squared his shoulders and Munchie Trot, knowing what he had to do, broke into a gentle jog and caught up with the rest of the group.

Even a flub-up (failing to report a friend's drinking) brought the Bonnie Prince greater honor, as he was shipped off to the finest prep school to see the world and escape the day-to-day distractions of living with a widowed mother who did not always want or choose to function as a mother should. His graduation from Harvard would be celebrated and his bride a true beauty with whom he joyfully shared his salad days at Virginia. A promising new career as a well-connected lawyer only completed the package, affirming the notion that with seemingly little effort—certainly no pain suffered, no forced exile—even as the youngest, he would be king. At least, his life appeared easy and sure to our discarded princess, who was much too busy on the ground—having been pushed from the nest so heartlessly, she thought—to look up at the last wee chick, peeking his head over the edge, so high up, cloistered in the branches, yet so all alone.

Re-Enter The Discarded Princess

Well, this was to be the story of Princess Number One, who is now buried deep in the deck as our tale moves along quickly with the queen's new life and the installation of the younger prince as king-to-be, and I can tell, as all writers know, that the narrative is rollicking away from our main character. Not for long, however; the discarded princess, like her royal ancestors, got busy, put her shoulder to the plow, and set to it. Would you, her grandchildren, not give her at least a small cheer of encouragement?

How can I say this? She went a little overboard. Was she simply outrageous or just a little insane? the neighbors pondered. They never guessed that she was bewitched.

She did, however, have her prince, who was a doctor besides. And Dr. Prince was just that—a prince made from the finest mold. He was from an outstanding family in South Carolina. His uncle had been the famous FBI agent Melvin Purvis, who in 1934 shot Dillinger and was on the cover of every newspaper and magazine in America and abroad. His grandfather, not his great-grandfather, was the most renowned Civil War veteran of Chester County. Dr. Prince grew up in a large brick house with stately columns. His cousins would become textile executives, chemists, and physicians. Uncles published scholarly dissertations; several relatives won the Pulitzer Prize. When the discarded

THE LATHANS

princess discovered Dr. Prince was Phi Beta Kappa, the deal was sealed. The princess had only to move to Chester, South Carolina, and her reign as queen would have been secure.

But something didn't sit right with the princess, and upstate South Carolina failed to beckon. Was it the food? Certainly Dr. Prince's mother tried. But the cakes and biscuits had been ordered days in advance, the peas were Le Sueur, and the eggs were cooked in too much bacon grease for a princess who not only wanted to rule, but who—yes, like her mother—wanted to parade around in elegant clothes. There were the fabulous artichoke-pickle relish and the perfect cornbread dressing, but somehow they were not enough. Dr. Prince's mother was, like all of the family, honorable, intelligent, hard-working Southern gentry and always sweet and kind. Yet the princess couldn't breathe. Get me out of here! And Dr. Prince did.

Thus the discarded princess again returned to Atlanta to face impossible obstacles and to attempt to reclaim a crown. As her mother before her, she now had two daughters and eventually a son. And like her father, she relentlessly began a regime to transform them into spectacular. These new little princesses never got to rest a minute. They were lugged to lesson after lesson, activity after activity, and stimulation after stimulation. They would attend the best schools, have the best teachers, make the best grades, be the outstanding leaders. Why didn't the princess leave them alone and let them just be their beautiful selves? Her own mother, the queen, had certainly preached that course of action with the conviction of a Billy Graham: "Just as I am, Lord. Just as I am."

The discarded princess refused to listen. She would do it her way. If she couldn't be queen, then she would be a fantastic mother whose children would be crowned. At the very least, she would embrace her children with one stretching hug as a loving mother should.

We have already alluded to the impossibility of the equal distribution of money. The distribution of a mother's love into equal parts is an even more impossible quest. But just as Brer Rabbit kept pleading, "Please don't throw me into that Briar Patch," the one place on earth he knew best and loved the most, so I say to you, "Take my hand, and let's jump into that maze of brambles and see the discarded princess as a mother and a wife."

What will we learn as we look for her love in action? Certainly do not expect to find love divided neatly into equal portions. Could it be that love is not a piece of pie or even a feeling, after all? Rather, it is a place where life abides…even among the briars.

Meet The Children

The discarded princess was sure that her firstborn would take up the quest to become queen and rule with the equanimity and grace she herself had failed to achieve. It didn't happen. The firstborn was studious, smart, and very beautiful, but she didn't like to raise her hand when she knew the answer. Though she was a talented athlete, team sports and the rank of captain held no allure. She was fiercely competitive and very original but focused on pumpkin-carving and birthday-card design, not things for which one would acquire fame and fortune. Artist Princess thrilled the family with her imagination one moment, only to wreck all three cars the next. She would ride the Mardi Gras float and win, but she thought of it as an art project, not as an affirmation to reign. One morning when she was forbidden to wear her father's paisley pajamas to the very strait-laced school, she dissolved into tears and refused to comply. She would never give in to easy convention. She had seen the magic dust and would dine on it forever. This was not a charm that only the dawn could break. The Artist Princess was an enchantment unto herself. She was determined to succeed—to be what her heart desired. Her creation of the "Shoe Box" as her essay for Brown not only got her in but was spoken of in such far-away places as Tanzania and Belize. At Brown she excelled, not just with her art, but academically, graduating magna cum laude, a feat no one in her family's illustrious academic history had achieved. Today her art work is hung in major museums and treasured by renown collectors. Could it be that one should not always listen to one's mother?

The second-born daughter, Play-Maker Princess, as the first, held on relentlessly to her life choices, refusing at every turn to select the path the discarded princess had so carefully imagined for her. This little princess had a head of beautiful blond curls, which she tossed fearlessly about; the curls and her tight group of friends were her armor and shield. She was always chosen to be the star, whether it was the lead in the first-grade play or senior class president. She was perfect to rule as queen, but the discarded princess had already assigned that role to the first-born sister and so was blind to any clues to the contrary. Miscasting has never stopped a blond, however. Impediments might get in her way, but she never wasted time examining them too carefully. She just skipped ahead. If you passed her the ball, you could always count on her to pass it along or safely pass it back. People trusted her competence, and she took success in her stride. She did it all with very little help. Independently, she would be the first to parade in a homecoming court, first to live in a London palace, first to land the perfect job, first to find a prince with fifth-generation First Presbyterian credentials, first to return home to give her mother solace. The discarded princess never understood how her child could be so successful and still have time to nurture her. Should not the roles have been reversed?

The little prince was yet another complete surprise, as different from his older siblings as they were from each other. His arrival had been an unexpected blessing, and while the discarded princess would never express such thoughts in public, the birth of a son was one of the most perfect moments in her life. The sisters adored him. As a mother, the discarded princess worked night and day, surrounding him with proper knights as playmates and assuring his attendance in the most rigorous training camps and clinics. His best coaches turned out to live next door, so training was available seven days a week and into the night. When things were looking a little blurry for his future, she even bought him a Labrador Retriever, the only dog for a gentleman and scholar, if not for a king. He acted out the part to the letter. He was a star athlete, good-looking, surrounded by friends, a class officer, in the right advanced placement classes, always keeping the family laughing and entertained. He leapt at the chance to attend a king-producing college. Alas, the discarded princess had failed to heed the most important part of her own insight…he acted out the part to the letter.

It was, in fact, an Academy Award-winning performance, for this child had no intention of being a king. He had chosen acting instead—comedy to be exact—and it would be to the stage that he would strive, not to the throne. His determination matched that of his older sisters, and he would never waiver. His coat of arms will surely read, "Preparare theatrati." Will you laugh or will you cry? You will be riveted to your seat, no matter what, for the performance will be spellbinding.

The children were outstanding; the discarded princess, as a mother, not so. She dressed the girls in matching dresses for holidays, but they were as different as night and day. She insisted her son wear Polo, wrestling him to the ground to put it on, while, mocking her vengeance with his own, he always struggled successfully to tear it off. He would be his own person, not just fit in. The discarded princess worked diligently cooking wonderful dishes, as she remembered her mother had done, only to be too worn out at dinner to rave about what the children had accomplished or to call out *Wordly Wise* with very much enthusiasm. She attended every game, not hiding quietly in the bushes as her father had done, but yelling and screaming the children on with every kick or random basket.

And do not forget the time at Pike Nurseries when, as she reached down to select a new plant, she let go of the wagon into which the children had jumped. That wagon with its precious cargo began to roll and quickly gathered speed on the steep slope, rolling, rolling, rolling under a moving tractor trailer truck, still going, going, and going until it reached the bottom of the hill, thank goodness not the highway. If you can't trust your mother to hold onto you, whom can you trust?

On and on she continued to struggle to be another, better mother, ironically following in the exact steps her own mother had trod. If that was not bad enough, after mocking her mother's dream of a garden, our little discarded princess worked just as hard, if not harder, than the queen to transform her yard into the garden of gardens. It was backbreaking work, but she thrived on it, for she had heard often enough "…such gardens are not made by singing:—'Oh how beautiful!' and sitting in the shade."

Surely, though, the garden was her own dream and not a borrowed one. Or did those very dirty garden gloves just help keep those sweating hands busy and hidden from view. Whatever the reason, a garden was a dream from which she could never escape.

She joined every social organization possible, and she still waved those uncontrollable hands, volunteering for any position. She did every task with as much enthusiasm as you can imagine, considering the fact that she was also working furiously in the yard, hauling trees and rocks, actively gathering the neighbors together at any opportunity, baking some difficult yet delicious new recipe, shuffling the little princesses and prince to all their activities, and trying to become a tennis star, a marathoner, a golfer, and a whatever else seemed important at time. All this and with the dinner ready and the make-up on when the doctor returned each night. The neighbors took her in stride—the insanity and outrageous behavior—because her pound cake was delicious, and she was their energy source, always trying to be available and free. I think they enjoyed the show.

THE RE-ENTRY

Peachtree Road Race Competitors

Take A Hike

You have now met the main characters. You know their considerable foibles. Within the constraints of this fairy tale with mythic allusions, delusions, and illusions intertwined, a look at this family's daily life might give us the insight we want. You can be assured there were unbelievable tests to address; incredible sorcerers, witches, ogres to meet or avoid; and many dangerous journeys to endure. Their trials and tribulations, in this basically twentieth-century tale, may be understood best under the simple heading "hike."

The word "hike" probably has as many different meanings as there are different childhoods. For you, today's reader from far-flung places, "Take a hike" might be translated as "Get lost" or "Leave me alone" in my urban wilderness filled with electronics, gadgets, and beeping buttons. For the discarded princess, the word "hike" was like a transcendental ode dedicated to long walks in the woods, mixed with stories told by her father of his solitary treks through north Georgia and North Carolina. A hike was a poem consisting of vanished Cherokees, clear streams, wild turkeys, pieces of mica sparkling in the dirt. On the other hand, for Dr. Prince, a "hike" was wedded in his memory to summer camp, where as a son whose father had died when he was but three, a hike meant a time and place when one is surrounded by men and lost boys. A hike was an adventure on which he became the leader, that camper who traveled the most difficult trails, chalked up the most miles, the Indian brave himself. For their children, the word hike grew to mean a giant tornado that gathered every single memory of childhood into a powerful swirling mass of endless odysseys and miles and miles of walking.

The list of hikes is legion. There was "LeConte," childhood, which actually was fun with the Reeses and Means. Who wouldn't love the bear cubs on the the path and oversized pancakes at dawn? There was "Pisgah," the bitter-sweet, where the Lathans and the Howards all joined together to hold hands around the world's largest tulip poplar tree, never imagining what anguish would later rent that circle apart. And "Arcadia Maine," Walden Pond, where the popovers took center stage in spite of Dr. Prince's constant repeating of "Boobies, the Boobies, look at the Boobies." Then there was "Mount Washington, New Hampshire," a tax deduction, but as most deductions at that time, one that proved more complex and dangerous than expected, as the crosses they saw through the mists when they finally reached the summit were real crosses marking where the deceased had been found after the blizzard of some other year.

There was "Thanksgiving Day," lost and found, when they literally lost the boyfriend that had come to dinner, and only the new son-in-law could find the way down. There were hikes in the rain and hikes through the brutal heat. There were hikes whose distances far exceeded what any child should have trekked. There was "Lake Solitude Grand Tetons, Wyoming," woman, where in the unimagined snow of August, the girls (who included a female moose) finally lured their father down in time to catch the last ferry back to civilization. Oh, my goodness, the hikes. They went to far and distant places, from the jungles of Costa Rica to the avenue of the Champs-Elysees. Every single experience brought more challenges than the one before, new impossible tests to be faced and subdued.

"Grand Canyon," majestic, stands out as the great summation. In many ways, it was the perfect hike. Reasoning that leaving for the West on Christmas Day would yield a purer, simpler Christmas, knowing full well how dreadful many of the other hikes had been, and prepared at least with proper shoes and coats, the family once more looked forward to a trip to witness one of the major sights of our America—the Beautiful—and to take a safe and short hike. Grand Canyon was a tourist site after all. Surely it wouldn't be transformed into something else. They were all experienced now. They knew what they were committing to. They had been on enough hikes to know. Of course, no one really had any idea what descending to the bottom of the Grand Canyon would entail or what getting back up on the icy trail would require, but then again, they never did.

As they began their descent, no one worried about or questioned either the map or the map reader, as the trail was clearly marked. No one commented on how difficult it was to keep your footing on the narrow, twisting trail through the slick ruts while simultaneously avoiding the many mule pats left from the day before. No one pushed or poked his sister or brother just for the pure devilment of it or ran ahead to pretend to be lost only to jump out with a shriek later. Everyone was older now. No one noted how few people they'd actually seen on the trail or how the time it was taking far exceeded original estimates. No one said a word in blame when it was discovered that the visitors center at the bottom was closed and, thus, no food or water available. No one complained when the red, yellow, purple, and quite glorious sides of the canyon began to take on darker and darker hues or when the temperature started to drop precipitously as minutes turned to hours and morning into late, then later, afternoon. No one mentioned that the trip up always takes twice as long as the trip down. No one began to fantasize about how great food, any food, even one cracker, would taste or how divine the prospect of a hot bath had become. No one danced a victory dance when they finally climbed out—after nine hours—and slowly made their way to the national park canteen to sit down at last. No one was surprised that none were able to move or lift their feet even one more time when the canteen staff closed the doors for the night. They all just sat immobilized, united, frozen. No one even said, "Never again," or "Over my dead body," in protest. What would be the point? They had survived this one. More would come, more challenges, more simple hikes transformed into great tests of physical endurance and pain. They all had what it took and would forevermore.

Then, finally, they laughed.

Yes, the swirling tornado that was their life was too much. Yes, there should have been some way for it to fall in place more easily than it did. Yes, the discarded princess pushed too hard to get out of the deck of cards in which she had been buried. But in spite of the hauling, the relentless moving something to somewhere else, the forever-trying, everyone seemed to be thriving. And if our princess had dared stop for even one minute, she might have seen all the glorious blessings pouring down around her. Instead, she saw more fields to plow, more slights to harbor, more things of which she could be jealous.

I wish there had been just a small bell tinkling every time one of those myriad blessings fell into her lap. It would have been so lovely to hear the ringing, like little silver bells heard in the distance, softly repeating, at the end of each day, day after day, year after year. Instead, our discarded princess was exhausted and fell asleep each night long before she could have heard this quiet night music. It would have been nice if she had.

And yet, there were blessings that our princess did joyfully celebrate. There was the wonderful yellow house at 1175 W. Brookhaven Drive; her prince, Dr. Prince; her beautiful, beautiful children; the delightful and ever-needed friends. And there was Jello.

Jello

We have spoken about money and class. The next difficult topic we must explore is that of race relations, segregation, and civil rights. This is a story which takes place in the South largely during the 1950s, 60s, and, 70s, and you have already learned that the discarded princess was very much in the midst of it, as tangled up as anyone in the complications and contradictions. Our discarded princess had the added perspective of the educated liberal elite, but she was also well aware of the huge gap between what people say and what people actually feel, whether they be northern or southern. Sadly, I must report to you that any justification for anything she did or failed to do will never be sufficient. Her only guides remain these three questions: How does one subdue each day (it is a daily battle) one's own prejudices and preconceptions? How does one summon up the courage needed when injustice stares one in the face? How does one ask for forgiveness when one fails?

There was nothing at first glance that told you what a blessing Jello was. She was certainly not grand nor tall nor stately, and she walked with a crooked gait due to the rickets she had suffered as a child growing up on a farm in Monroe County. She spoke in short sentences, never telling long, rhythmic stories nor sharing wandering insights from her past. She had one son named Bobby who drove a long black cadillac, but she rarely spoke of her private life. She smiled often, but it was always a reserved smile, with one gold tooth shining forth, and only because she knew that her smile made you feel better. She did not particularly like to cook but would if needed, and certainly there were never any heavenly angel-food-cake secrets she was going to share.

 She was uncomfortable taking messages and was frankly too busy to answer the phone anyway. She didn't like going to the door when the bell rang, even when it was her sister, Belle, who worked down the street. She couldn't stop to visit. She never put all the socks in the right drawers. But she was a wonder at her work. Everyone was impressed by her, even the Tiger-Eyed Princess, who employed German nannies and handsome, gray-haired butlers. Even the queen was a little envious of the magnificent Jello.

 The princess's knowledge of Jello's life was scant, but from what the princess could gather, Jello was her real name; it was on her Social Security card. Still, Belle, her sister, affectionately called her Jean. The whole neighborhood saw Jello walk to work three days a week, making the long trek from MARTA, and everyone wished they knew someone as loyal. She had her routine down perfectly, attacking all the mess—the sink heaped with dirty dishes from the night before, the unmade beds, the clothes thrown everywhere, Dr. Prince's piles of papers. She didn't quit until everything was back in order, the floors shining, the ironing crisp and spotless, the dishwasher empty. The pillows were always back on the sofa, the towels were folded just right. She kept the princess supplied with starched linen dresses and polished silver. She even filled the vases with magnolia leaves without being asked. But that devotion, her work ethic, that gift for housekeeping was not really what made Jello so wonderful.

Jello had something that was not for hire. She kept our discarded princess going. Jello was everything the princess was not, so the princess held tightly to her. It was Jello who was filled with grace, not some wispy fluff of grace that could be blown about by the wind, but that rock solid strong saving grace. She never questioned the princess's boundless energy and struggle. When our princess was suddenly eaten up with jealousy, Jello would give her a sharp look, which said in no uncertain terms, "What are you thinking?"

When the princess was too tired to move or struck dead by a stomach virus, it was Jello who turned down the bed, smoothed the sheets, and said, "Lie down a minute, and I will keep it quiet for a while." It was Jello who cleaned up after all the princess's numerous disasters and Jello who was there when the children came home and the princess was still out battling a tennis ball. It was Jello who could find all the lost pieces of this-and-that, whatever the still growing family had managed to lose. On the other hand, it was always Jello who was blamed if you could not find your other shoe.

I hope there is someone who will look after you the way that Jello looked after the discarded princess and her family. Pundits may insist that you must do it alone. They are partly right. Still, I believe everyone needs some help doing the physical part of life. The physical world is very real. It will crash in on you and beat you down. "Tired to the bone" is as much an impediment to success as lack of talent or money. More than great wealth, more than a fleet of cars, more than the grandest of castles, you will need another hand, whoever it may be. As with our princess, your mother may not be the one. Even your grandmother, even your spouse. Most expect their mothers, certainly their grandmothers, to be the foundations—steady, sure, ready, and constant. Often it just doesn't happen that way. Royalty seem to have a knack for finding a source, and you will need the kind of help that best suits your own life. But if your life is to be filled with the richness that comfort can bring, you will need someone—or perhaps many people—next to you, beside you, and behind you with the quiet, solid grace of Jello.

The Princess And The Pea

The story now turns to a central scene. It is a bedroom in a castle. Mattresses are piled on the bed, almost to the ceiling. The guest, a princess, yet to be recognized, is lying on top, but rather than resting, she is tossing and turning, unable to sleep. A pea has been planted, the smallest of tiny peas, under the bottom-most mattress. The princess, so sensitive and pure, cannot bear even the small intrusion of this tiny irritant, which for our princess, is the incessant wish to be recognized.

The discarded princess had simply read this story too many times, believed it too completely, piled too many mattresses on top. Would anyone finally just say, "Stop. We know who you are. A princess after all. Welcome."? Or would the princess climb down and simply remove the silly pea? In fact, years passed. And the mattresses continued to amass. Where is the fairy godmother for goodness' sake?

A fairy godmother? Exactly. The princess did need a fairy godmother, and finally, one did show up. She was a little late on the scene, don't you think? But she did have the power—she knew all about magic. But one had to buy the ticket to get into her house. She did not exactly swoosh into yours, as it says in the book. Her name was Sheila McQue.

The Fairy Godmother Arrives

The discarded princess had expected a fairy godmother with at least a few grand excesses, help to give in the kitchen, and hopefully a Zip-a-Dee-Doo-Dah or two. She would have preferred that her fairy godmother be round and soft around the edges with pink tulle petticoats and ribbons flying in the wind. Instead, this fairy godmother spoke with a crisp English accent and was highly disciplined and restrained; her gray curls were held tight as if bound with bobby pins. She dressed in navy blue and winked one eye if you repeated one of her charms correctly or laughed at her rather dry jokes. Nothing happened after the wink, though you might wait expectantly.

In her presence, you were transported to an England where bedrooms are named for flowers, fine linens accompany your tea, daffodils bloom in the garden, and toast with marmalade is served for you and me. However, she was not your godmother of choice if you were looking for jeweled tiaras, crenellated castles, mysterious strangers, or a life of ease. This godmother dealt more in bits and pieces, things perishable, often inexpensive, and quite plain.

When the discarded princess first entered her enchantment, the princess was frankly taken aback. For one who loved broad, sweeping gestures, large bunches of this and that, more and more of whatever it was and piled high, a godmother who forced you to reuse tiny stems of freesia cut down to just the nubs surely seemed to lack the powers one might need and certainly was depending on. No, this godmother, Sheila McQue, was more a godmother of sea glass and broken dreams carefully collected into a glass vase, turning from green to turquoise through layers of splintering light. Her creations were like birds' nests, both strong and soft, artfully constructed with leftover twigs assembled into a rhythm somehow complete. Whatever her arrangement, something wild was always added…not wild as in reckless but wild as in free.

One could not have ordered a better godmother for our discarded princess. When Sheila McQue waved a wand, the princess finally started paying attention to the bits and pieces that were caught in the frantic folds of her whirling dervish life. "Take care," this godmother said. "Prepare. Watch over. Insignificant will often steal the stage. Add something gathered from your garden or stolen from the roadside if you dare. That is where the magic lies."

However, regardless of the grace-filled days, the countless blessings, the successful husband, and the oh-so-beautiful three children, even with a magical British fairy godmother to show her how, in spite of all of it, our princess was still on a mission to take her rightful place. For those just observing, everything did seem to be on track, moving along with breakneck speed, going somewhere, when suddenly the earth shook and the ground opened wide and our princess fell—down, down, down a horrible black hole. You did not see this coming, I bet, and neither did she.

Be alert and ready for such a fall, my dears. It was not in a deep, dark forest—in the forest, you are ready. Had not every fairy tale prepared her to never go into the woods alone and to always be on the lookout for a cunning wolf or bewitched messenger? Had not every hike and journey been but a practice so that she would be prepared, ready, and watchful for a drop off a cliff, a crack in the earth, a snake coiled in the grass? Doesn't the music always warn you that something terrible is about to happen so that you can gird yourself in armor and gather the knights? No, if I remember correctly, there were no warning chords or appropriate foreboding flourishes.

The Blackness

The blackness comes. It may come early in your life, it may come late. It may come fast, it might come slowly. It will come in different shades and has many moving parts. It is not a test, a challenge, a journey. It is just emptiness for which there are no words.

When the fairy godmother looked down into the dark cavern, she could only say, "Poor child, I am so sorry. My magic is helpless now. Magic is perception and works only in the light. It is too dark where you are falling." And then she disappeared.

To understand the all of it, you must listen carefully, for this blackness is as much a part of any true fairy tale as is the magic dust or moonlight. Look down into the emptiness, but do not get too close to the edge. Perhaps a flashlight might help you see at least the shadows. The shadows are but half of what was transpiring, but seeing them will be sufficient enough for you to understand what happened to our princess and how this blackness shapes our tale.

At first, it was like the night of a nuclear disaster.

The field of medical practice was on the brink of catastrophic change, at least from the point of view of an internist, and the ramifications of this change were affecting everything with which our energetic family had to deal. Dr. Prince had bet on one strategy to succeed (work hard, be an outstanding physician, and everything would fall into place), and now that plan had to be tossed. You could be an excellent physician, but if you did not play by certain rules, ones you did not make or even know about, you were out. And even if you did figure out what the rules were, payment would be at least six months later and only a fraction of what you had billed.

The only solution proposed was technology, but as computers were barely up and running and specialized software nonexistent and all beyond a solo practitioner's budget anyway, most doctors were frozen in some kind of terrorized state with not a glimmer of how to proceed. They were not only stmied, but they were also divided by some unseen formula in the sky as to who would get what of the meager insurance reimbursements. All this pitted internists against surgeons—who had once worked together closely and certainly depended on each other—and everyone against the hospital (now the only source of expertise or capital or bargaining power). Even the ailing patients began to doubt what the doctor advised them to do. In the meantime, this family had grown to five, the private school bills were growing, college was looming, everyone needed a car, and the yellow house was always there demanding another coat of paint. Would they have to let Jello go?

Our princess just kept moving. She quickly finished her master's degree in art history, which at first had been meant only for her queenly resume but became a necessity for getting some kind of a job. She actually did get a position, thanks to a friend's help and really quite appropriate for one who plans to live in a castle one day, as administrator of the Swan House. She gave it her all. It has been my experience that jobs you like do not usually pay very well; and although she did receive appropriate raises, her salary barely made a dent in the radioactive oozing of insufficient earnings. She did learn some very valuable lessons about what workers really want, how dangerous inter-departmental jealousies can be, and what it is like to be treated as if you are invisible, but all in all, in spite of her heroic efforts, the nuclear disaster was not abated. It oozed on.

It became clear the princess was going to have to get a real job or, rather, work in Dr. Prince's office and see if she could figure out what the rules were and how the technology worked. Everyone agreed the doctor had enough to do just being a doctor. Well, I confess to you as family, the people in charge of Katrina or the Japanese tsunami recovery had nothing on the princess in terms of heaping disaster on top of a disaster.

It was more than ludicrous. The first thing she did was to flood the office below when she left the water running while giving the office a thorough cleaning. She couldn't even mop up the lake now in the break room because she had scathingly fired the laundry service, which charged exorbitant amounts for unused linens—only a few paper towels remained.

Next, she threw out a month or two of Medicare reports because the paper they were printed on was, like the paper one gets from some failed land deal or fraudulent publishing house, surely well below the standards of what our government would use for something as important as the nation's health care.

And then it became necessary to retire the only employee who really knew anything about how to run the office, which bills it was time to pay, who delivered what, and whether the diagnosis was for a common cold or a life-threatening flu. This job was definitely not what the princess had planned in her dream to rule as queen one day. The skills needed were not her skills. She hated all of it—not just not-having-a-clue but having to get people to pay their bills and show up for appointments, paying for printer ink, working machines, and having to keep perfect records of every single thing.

All she wanted was to don one of those surgical masks and lower her head to hide her failure and incompetence. Her only cover was that no one else, not even brilliant surgeons or the most skilled administrators, had any idea how to adapt and change. And thank the Lord she was a woman—even better the wife of a physician—so her mistakes were chalked up to inexperience and her insights overlooked, giving her time to pull it off. And pull it off they did. Dr. Prince was finally on board, having abandoned his Fox News rhetoric. Within a year or two, there was a six-figure difference, and the good doctor was still practicing the high-quality, careful medicine he had sworn to do. Even so, the seepage persisted, and all the while, a tsunami was on the way, ready to crash into the shore.

Now the tsunami, which came next, was yet another shade of the blackness. This tsunami was not a giant tidal wave of ocean water. It was a liquid in a bottle—or a barrel, to put it more accurately—and it swept over them with the same force as any great storm, with waves higher than rooftops and a vengeance you cannot imagine. It turned over cars, rerouted their lives, filled hospital beds, and impacted their personal debt. It was a miracle no one died, although some did come close—too close.

The family searched out the leading wizards in their field. What are you so afraid of? they asked. Why is alcohol so important in your lives? Where's your courage? they questioned.

The wizards were too young and too earnest to see how seductively alcohol had been woven into the myths of Southern life, at the same time being a coiled serpent ready to poison anyone who dared say "Do" or "Don't." How is one to know what was just unnecessary worry or impending doom? How does one separate the control freak from the astute observer? Can one recognize what is the real thing, not a breeze blowing in from the east, but a storm bringing all the power and fury of total destruction? There was nowhere to hide, and so this royal family did proceed—one day at a time—as you are supposed to do with alcohol. With the help of wizards from the West, they at least got through the disaster (or so they hoped). They were told this was the whole family's issue and to expect a miracle, and that is what they did. They banded together and expected.

And then, in the midst of the nuclear night that was medicine and the tsunami's savage fury that was alcohol, our princess felt a strange, visceral tingling all over; everything was shifting. And then the earth itself moved, cracking open, and down into the darkness our discarded princess tumbled, her arms waving madly. This time there was nothing to hang onto, no magic dust or quick wit to brighten up a dire situation with answers and humor. There was no grace in place to soften the fall, because there seemed to be no bottom. The only thing worse than the falling and the blackness was the thought that the great jaws would soon crash back together, crushing our princess like a bug. She would not go out in flames, she would go out as ash.

It was a mix more toxic than the many pains of adolescence, more unbearable than not being chosen, more paralyzing than the dreaded pollo, sadder in its loneliness than being discarded. There were no prayers to float up to heaven. There was no music playing. Only silence, broken by her scream, and then silence again. There was no way out. Imagination was helpless. The king was dead. The dreaming stopped. Nothingness takes all.

The Tiger-Eye Princess To The Rescue

You all have been waiting so patiently to hear more about the beautiful Tiger-Eyed Princess. Now, don't you think, is the time to bring her back into our story.

Who among us doesn't love to hear tales of lavish parties, Zonnie Sheik jewels, great adventures of historic proportions, life from the top, a fairy tale come true? Even with just a few asides, precise details of the little mischiefs that befall the most illustrious of the wealthy are ten times more entertaining than all this struggle, both real and imagined, that our family had to face. And tell these tales our Tiger-Eyed Princess could. The Tiger-Eyed's stories were diamond studded, bright, and incandescent, because she was there, front row and center, looking beautiful, full of life and excitement, always delivering the punch line perfectly as her audiences remained rapt and silent.

Let's consider just one anecdote, titled "What I did for Atlanta and the Bid for the 1996 Olympics," in order to see how captivating her stories are compared to the very dark tales with which this narrative has become absorbed.

What I Did For Atlanta And Its Olympic Bid

In the late 1980s, a few Atlantans came up with the preposterous idea that Atlanta could win the bid to be an Olympic city. Such a vision would require more than the usual imagination. It was as if these citizens—like those Westminster students with their Mardi Gras floats—believed that the impossible could happen. (Funny, looking back, I realize more than half of that committee had participated in the Westminster Mardi Gras tradition and so knew what was involved, both the good and the bad. Anyway, you remember that I urged you to hold onto the belief that the impossible is possible.)

It soon became clear that the city's chances of winning would be greatly increased if Atlanta, with its outstanding central location, was also a coastal city with a little historical charm. The discarded princess was solicited to ask her sister for a small favor.

The Tiger-Eyed Princess was always so generous, loved to help, and for sure had more imagination than most of the state of Georgia, so it was easy for the discarded princess to give her a call. As the princess remembers, the exchange went like this:

"Tiger-Eyes, would it be possible for you to host a small luncheon for the top brass of the International Olympic Committee, including only the most famous of the famous, mostly their wives? They would be flown down by private jet to Camelot, South Carolina, by the sea, and it should not take more than a morning of your time."

"Of course, I would love to," Tiger-Eyes immediately responded. "My house is always ready. It's easy to set up tables on the veranda." Then she started getting into it. "Let's see. I'll borrow a limousine from somewhere and dress everyone up in a uniform. We'll get Tom from the museum to give a short, entertaining history of Camelot as we tour the city. The food will be home-cooked specialties, fresh crab, Huguenot torte. This will be fun! And I love doing something for my old hometown—Atlanta. Can you get me opening ceremony tickets?"

The plans grew more elaborate, both on her end and on the Atlanta Bid Committee's, but always she kept her good cheer. The group of visitors was ceremoniously taken from the airport and wined and dined (although dined is somewhat of an exaggeration as the international wives wore size two and thus did not exactly eat). In the Tiger-Eyed Princess's telling of the experience, she here adds, as only she can, in a fake, all-encompassing foreign accent, that all the women from the great capitals around the globe began to chant, "Shoes.....Bob Ellis, Bob Ellis, Bob Ellis... shoes." It was in quest of shoes that the wives of the International Olympic Committee came to the shores of Camelot, not, it seemed, to see the great, expansive sports arena that is the Atlantic.

Thus, all preparations for the subtle revealing of an ocean view (it had not been easy to transport acres of Atlantic coastline inland about three-hundred miles) and all stellar attempts to blend serious espionage with gracious hospitality were interrupted by women's universal need to shop. Thank goodness the Tiger-Eyed Princess knew the Bob Ellis store well and wanted to go too. Atlanta won the bid.

Now, when the discarded princess attempts to tell any one of her many stories about the Olympics—about entertaining the Guatemalans at the more humble 1175 West Brookhaven Drive, housing the entire UNC Phi Delt pledge class for the duration, trading pins with Clinton's swat team, or volunteering for hours—she finds too many details to relate, too many nuances and hurdles to explain, and no matter where the story starts, she somehow always tries to drag you through the bombing one more time. "It was such a great testament to the Atlanta spirit, etc., etc., etc." I'm not even going to retell one of her stories, because you all already know what I mean. The Tiger-Eyed Princess would always reign as queen and deservedly so. Her short, carefully crafted tales are gems. Who really wants to know everything anyway?

Compassion

In fact, we have kept the Tiger-Eyed Princess in the background for too long. We need that soft ocean breeze, which she seems to carry with her, to come blowing in and move this story gently toward its conclusion.

So, to resume, in the life of the discarded princess, the blackness was everywhere, an all-encompassing nothingness spreading like contagion, but thank goodness the Tiger-Eyed Princess called.

Here's what the discarded princess remembers her saying: "M, I have a wonderful idea. The other M has just gotten a divorce and needs cheering up. Why don't you both come to Camelot for a little R & R? You can stay in our newly renovated guest house. We can shop, see gardens, and treat ourselves to delightful lunches. Bring one of your elegant pantsuits, and we will get the latest shoes. Please come! We will have so much fun, and I need you to help make the other M laugh."

Yes, the Tiger-Eyed Princess was in full force. With her creative juices flowing, a great sense of flair, and an innate, ever-sensitive kindness, the Tiger-Eyed Princess was going to rescue our princess.

And so our discarded, devastated princess did go. First, she bought a new Piazza Sempione; then she washed the car and headed to South Carolina. She cried most of the way there, switching from NPR to Willie Nelson, but somehow the road trip did help a little, and she was at least functioning enough to smile as she thought about the new outfit, in its crisp white paper, its price tags still on, lying ready in the back seat.

Believe it or not, they had a wonderful time. The Tiger-Eyed Princess, installed queen that she was, definitely knew how to rescue you in style. They shopped for art, they bought new shoes, they went click-clacking across the cobbled streets of the city, never missing a beat. They were entertained like visiting dignitaries, and the discarded princess fell asleep—a wonderful, natural sleep—on beautiful monogrammed sheets, starched just right. The weather cooperated, and the scent of jasmine was even more delicious than the home-cooked fried chicken and pimento cheese.

When the princess next met with the wizard who was in charge of bringing her back from the brink, he asked as she sat down, "How are things going?" Surprisingly, our princess replied, "You know, I feel better."

He smiled, as if he knew all along that she would eventually get her bearings.

"You do? What has happened?" And so our princess told him how much fun she had had in Camelot, how the Tiger-Eyed Princess had treated her like royalty, even though all humiliation was about to be heaped on her head, and how wonderful it had been waking up with that glorious seaside light pouring in the window.

His smile became more contemplative, and he said, "Well, finally, you have experienced it, experienced the one true thing in this world. You have received compassion. Once you know that compassion exists, that it reaches out and touches even you, you will be fine."

"What are you saying?" asked the princess. "Compassion?"

"Yes," he answered. "Compassion and mercy."

The princess did not get it. "How can that make everything right? What does compassion have to do with it? What does treating me royally, even though I am about to be turned to ash, have to do with it? Compassion from the Tiger-Eyed Princess? Have you not been listening to what I've been saying for the last year? Was it not the perfect smile of the Tiger-Eyed Princess that had bewitched everyone, so that the king thought none of the children needed braces, and I was stuck with my crooked teeth forever? Was it not because this Tiger-Eyed Princess was such a good athlete that I had to take a million tennis lessons? In the hot, broiling sun of the Florida Panhandle, did I not hit 300 lobs to her backhand only to have 301 come flying back at me?"

The wizard only nodded. "It usually happens that way. The one you least expect, the supposed enemy, the stranger, even the middle child, may be the person who may pick you up when you are truly down, carry you in their arms to the nearest inn, and leave directions as to your future care, secured by a gold coin placed in the innkeeper's palm."

"Oh," she interrupted, "I know the moral imperative to serve your fellow man, that do-good thing I never got the hang of, and it only made me feel worse."

"No, it is not a directive to wrap up every starving stranger you might see. It is instead a promise of how much you are loved. The imperative behind the promise is not to go about being Lady Bountiful but to open your heart so that you can feel the gift. And when you do feel that love, it will be all you will ever need. God in His mercy has made that promise to all. Your job is to keep your heart open to the stranger—maybe your sister, even to the enemy—because the stranger may be the very one about to bring what you need the most."

"You mean the only one true thing is a simple promise that, no matter what, someone cares?"

"You have it, more or less."

Now our princess did feel better, but it would take time for her to understand what had happened, and how it is that when you are down and out and someone picks you up, it can be the one true thing in a very complex and complicated world.

How can this simple promise possibly compete for attention when all the great thinkers have put forth so many other erudite, difficult to grasp theories? What does this compassion theory as the end-all tell us about how to deal with money, the inequities of inheritance, and the royal privilege of ruling with justice and wisdom? How does compassion address all our fears, the blackness, and the existence of evil? What about being the one who hits the ball back 301 times? What about being the one who captures the lingering looks? How does compassion explain away all that longing? Can it make you a better mother?

At the next visit, the wizard continued, "Don't you see? It is you who experienced the compassion, not the Tiger-Eyed Princess. The story of the Good Samaritan is really the story of promise to the lone traveler who fell among thieves. It is the traveler's story, not the Samaritan's. The traveler is the one who is rescued, carried gently to the inn, fed, and tenderly cared for. That is the promise to you."

"Yes, I do feel better. Are you sure it was compassion that changed everything? Where is my dream to be queen, to be the number-one princess, to be a striking beauty? What about getting even for all the wrongs received? What about forgiveness for the so many wrongs I perpetuated? How do I rid myself of the dream-shaking guilt, the source of which I do not even know?"

"That is the very subtle twist, or you might say the patina, the secret formula, the fizz. The promise is there, has always been there. Once you experience it, then it becomes your story to tell. You can tell it any way you choose. Add magic dust or spilled blood—perhaps a pinch of both. It's your recipe to stir. God has taken care of the most important part. You are loved, even adored. And if the Gospel writers included the part about gifting gold coins, maybe you should as well. Remember, experiencing the love comes with new possibilities but also with new opportunities. You have your own story, and compassion too is there to share. I hope you will—share the compassion—as you tell your tale.

And slowly it did unfold: a truly, wonderful, mysterious story and, best of all, it was her very own.

The True Story

Well, let's see…I guess I had better start from the beginning again, for each of you needs to know the true story of what happened to this not particularly significant family, your family from Georgia, who made their way, rocking and rolling, sometimes gloriously, sometimes not, through the chaos, tribulations, changes, joy, blackness, invention, evil, malaise, good fortune, and turned-up-side-down world that was the twentieth century.

Once upon a time in Georgia, there was a duchess who, odd as it sounds, wore a rather large hat and always dressed in gray.

What on earth was a duchess doing in Georgia of all places, and why in the world would anyone always wear gray?

Well, this duchess had royal connections there, and it was a cowboy wizard who put her in gray.

"Silver and gray look best on you," he said. "You will be smashing in red, if you dare to reveal who you are."

Surprisingly, the gray and silver did make her feel elegant, so she wore them often. And red too, sometimes, when she gathered up her courage. She carried a big, expensive-looking pocketbook, and if she ever dropped it (which, as a matter of fact, she often did) and everything came spilling out, you would surely see the strange contents it contained: a finely starched handkerchief, some wadded-up Kleenex, a pair of silver Manolo Blahniks (size

11), a torn but well-handled treasure map, a matchbook, a simple promise, and if you were lucky and looked carefully, you might see magic dust, catching the light and swirling, as magic dust often does, up, up into the air.

    What wonderful things happened next? Those, my children, are the stories for another day.

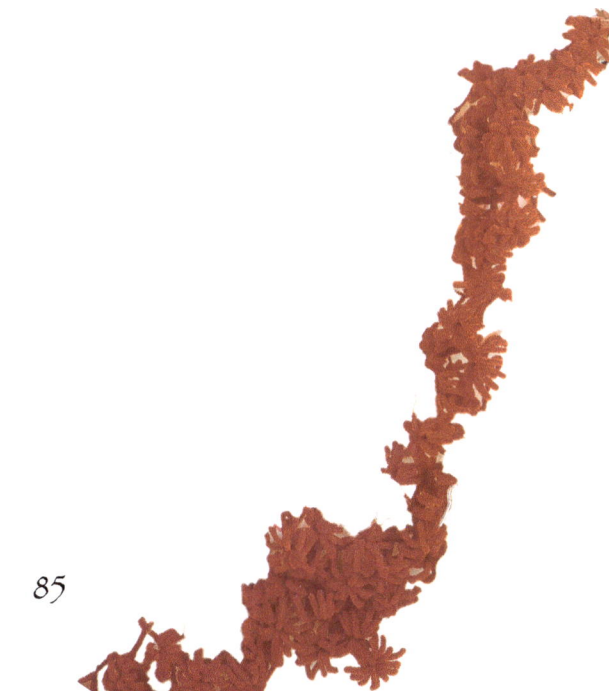

Bits And Pieces

As we close this book of family history and fairy tales, there is a little surprise—a gift for you. It is a collection, an odd assortment, stray things the duchess has picked up along her way, a few memories, something from her garden or her kitchen or perhaps foraged from the creek. It may not seem like much, but take a minute to look.

These reminiscences are just that—bits and pieces, separate, loose. Some are carefully guarded treasures, others jottings on yellowing paper, torn and folded, even snapshots. People from the duchess's long and unusual past make appearances. Several of these "bits" are simple recipes, because strangely, sometimes that is all that's left. Maybe "home-cooked" is the best gift anyway.

To appreciate your present fully, you need to examine each one of these pieces carefully, holding them, one at a time, up to the sun, or collecting a few together. Trying a bite here or mixing in a story of your own—you might just find a composition that holds delight. In any case, you will need these leftovers to make our history complete.

The gift is to pretend and play, and if that fairy godmother of bits and pieces happens to wave her wand, then these last few strands, these discarded and forgotten scraps, as if covered in magic dust, may suddenly catch fire and warm your heart.

The Reverend Frank Hudson and Princess Number One

Francis (always called Frank) Simmons Hudson
Father of the King

Papa Hudson was lean with beautiful white hair and mustache, but from what the princess could surmise, he did not have the respect of his son. Perhaps his son, our king, was unhappy that he had to provide his father and mother with a house when his father, a Methodist minister of the North Georgia Circuit, had no house to give him and had, in fact, never given him anything in particular. The only Christmas gifts our king remembered were an orange in the bottom of his sock and, another year, dried figs. He ate every one, every last fig, immediately that Christmas day and was so sick he missed all the week's festivities, if there were any. Other relatives have a much brighter memory of the preacher patriarch—of his gentleness, his sense of humor, his devotion to the church. Even the queen found a tender story from his past to retell.

Papa was the youngest of five children born to Eliza Dorsey and William Hudson. Both of his parents were from landed farmers, respected citizens of Hall and Jackson Counties. However, as did millions of other people on the move, passing through the Southern states of North Carolina, UpState South Carolina, and Georgia during the 1840s and '50s, the William Hudsons decided to leave their Georgia home to settle in Selina County, Arkansas. Not many details of life in Arkansas are known, but sometime about 1856, when Papa was still a baby, the Georgia Dorseys received the news that William Hudson had disappeared and that it didn't look like he was coming back.

John Dorsey, Eliza's father, immediately instructed his three sons to gather all the wagons and go bring Eliza and the children home. In only a few more years, the Civil War broke out, and no one, not even the top genealogical sleuths, were ever able to find any trace of William Hudson again.

When the queen told the tale of bringing Eliza home, she described in detail the hurried preparation for the long, dangerous trip across three states. "It must have been early August," the queen would say. "The summer crops gathered in and the cotton still ripening in the field. They would have to hurry to return in time to oversee the picking."

The wagons were painted green, and you could almost hear the chains rattle and clank as the teams were harnessed and hitched. The sons were excited and ready to go, while the anxiety of the mother and father only grew as they imagined the perilous journey ahead and the changes and sacrifices that were sure to follow. And the return must have been a sight to remember, the dust flying in billowing clouds, everyone hurriedly gathering on the porch for the homecoming. Surely the boys made it a grand entrance, the teams almost at a gallop; they were heroes after all. And I can imagine the comforting solace that Eliza felt—though I am sure, too, a relief mixed with fear one could taste—when she stepped down from the wagon, holding her baby son tight.

There was also the story from Papa's days as a pastor, a story printed in a newspaper (no one has a copy, but everyone swears it's true). Papa is said to have gone to the jail where they were holding Leo Frank. When a reporter approached, Papa Hudson said, "I think he is innocent." Because he was dismissed from his church for that statement, the family had to move again, in one year rather than in the usual two.

The duchess has a special memory of her visits with her grandfather. Papa Hudson would insist on giving her an old rusty teacup from a child's playset he had found in his yard. This ritual took place on every visit. Her grandfather would say, "I found something just for you," and untie the cup from the fence and offer it to her. Each time, she responded, "I don't want it." She could not bring herself even to pretend to accept such an insufficient gift.

At Wellesley, she used the rusty teacup as a metaphor for the refusal of love when it was somehow incomplete. The grade of A came with the comment, "This is the work of a real writer." Funny, isn't it, that the rusty teacup became one of her favorite treasures? I hope she is thanking her grandfather this very minute.

 Papa Hudson's Tea

Take a lost and rusty cup and sip imagined tea with your grandfather. It just might be the best you will ever have.

Mother Hudson's fine needlework

Mary Watts Hudson
Mother of the King

Mother Hudson was from a most illustrious family: the Bradfords of Halifax County, North Carolina. If you were to really attempt to claim a crown, her line would be the best one to follow back.

Mother Hudson was most famous for her beautiful needlework, which you can see in pictures of her children's dresses. None of the needlework remains, and I believe that whatever else was saved from the Bradfords and the Watts (her father's doctor's chest; love letters from the Civil War) was washed away in a Chattahoochee flood. Ask Lamar Roberts—he might know.

Mother Hudson's Orange Marmalade

This is her only recipe that has survived, but the queen felt it captured her personality perfectly: very frugal, hearty, and rather tart, but beloved by her son, and so it was the queen who saved it to pass along to you.

Makes 12 to 15 pints

The night before, put together into a large pot 6 to 8 whole oranges and 4 whole lemons, seeds removed, sliced as thinly as possible. Cover the fruit with 9 pints of water and let them soak for 10 to 12 hours. Boil the fruit and water hard for 45 minutes. Set aside for 10 to 12 hours.

Add 10 pounds of sugar to the pot and take it to a hard boil for 45 minutes. Add lemon juice if it's not tart enough. Put in jars, seal. Makes 12 to 15 pints.

◇ The Queen's Fudge ◇

Sadly, I must report there is no recipe for the fudge. If there were, the duchess would have made some this very morning, and that would have been your gift today. The recipe was probably not important anyway. It was the technique: when you took it off the stove, how you held the spoon as you were beating, recognizing the exact minute when you needed to stop to pour it onto the heavily buttered plate. The queen would never let anyone else try to do it, either. I think because, quite frankly, she knew how good she could make it, and by the time she had gone to all that trouble, she wanted a piece to eat right away. She was not going to eat some child's mistake.

The lack of a fudge recipe only fueled the duchess's desire to try to come up with something as wonderfully tasty as that fudge. The Outrageous Brownie Recipe belonged to the Tiger-Eyed Princess first, but our duchess made it her own simply by making it all the time. (If she lives a long, happy life, a diet of brownies will remain her secret. If she dies tomorrow, you will know why—but I will tell you she enjoyed these brownies as much as anything. She eats them every day.) It was the Tiger-Eyed Princess who met Lee Bailey in person. He came to her gracious home on Church Street, looking for great Southern fare from a good Southern cook. No matter who's on first, says the duchess, enjoy.

The Tiger-Eyed Princess's Recipe for Outrageous Brownies

(with a Few Modifications by the Duchess)

1 pound (4 sticks) of butter
1 pound plus 3 cups of semisweet chocolate chips
6 ounces of unsweetened chocolate
6 large eggs
2 tablespoons plus 1 ½ teaspoons of instant espresso
2 tablespoons of vanilla extract
2 ¼ cups of sugar
1 cup of all-purpose flour, sifted
1 tablespoon of baking powder
1 teaspoon of salt
5 cups of nuts (the duchess uses a combination of chopped walnuts and pecans)

Preheat the oven to 350 degrees. Grease and flour a 12-x-18-inch jellyroll pan. Set it aside.

In the top of a double boiler, melt together the butter, 2 3/4 cups of the chocolate chips, and the unsweetened chocolate until they are smooth. Set the melted mixture aside to cool to room temperature.

Gently combine the eggs, espresso, vanilla, and sugar, then stir this mixture into the cooled chocolate. Set the batter aside.

Sift together the flour, baking powder, and salt. Mix them into the cooled batter. Finally, fold in the remaining chocolate chips and the nuts. Pour the mixture into the greased pan.

Bake 20 to 25 minutes, just until the center of the mixture has puffed up. Do not over bake. Cut the brownies while they're still hot from the oven. Next, put the pan in the refrigerator to harden them before you re-cut. Store by freezing them.

The Queen's Treasured Secrets Quail

The queen was most proud of her quail recipe; again, though, it is really more of a technique, which she recited over and over and was happy to share.

Check fresh-killed, cleanly plucked quail for any leftover shot. Dust the bird lightly with flour, add plenty of salt and pepper, and brown it in butter and a little bacon grease in an iron skillet. Can you believe they made a special container just for saving bacon grease? Remove the quail from the pan.

This is the important part. The roux has to be just right. You make a roux by browning more flour in more butter in the iron skillet. The little specks that remain in the pan after you have browned the bird are the source of the rapture, so never throw the leftover pan juices away. The flour must turn dark, dark brown. This will take a lot of patience. Then, one millisecond before it turns black, you slowly add enough chicken stock to make a rather thin sauce.

Return the quail to the gravy. Cover the pan tightly, and simmer the dish. You must watch it carefully, and add stock as needed, until the quail is nicely steamed. Add lots of black pepper and cook until gravy is thick and delicious.

A hunting we shall go

◇ Creamed Fried Corn ◇

For Thanksgiving Day, it was the queen's job to bring the green beans and the fried corn. As she got older and just a little infirm, she cheated with the beans, very cleverly she thought, using a frozen version. However, she remained forever true to the fried corn.

The Silver Queen (I do not know how she got it in November!) you must hand-cut off the ear. Then with a sharp knife, scrape any remaining starch left on the ear into the pot with the whole kernels. Add butter (as much as you dare) and cook it in the iron skillet for a few minutes. You do not want to overcook it, but it needs to cook through. Add lots of salt and pepper and then a little milk to turn the starch into a creamy sauce.

Her most outstanding achievement had to be the peach ice cream, or the macaroni and cheese, though, frankly, everything tasted good. No wonder the king would never eat out.

New Year's Day's Turnip Greens and Black-eyed Peas

These are familiar to most everyone now that regional cooking is such a rage. But back in the 1950s, this strange ritual was a strictly Southern affair. As soon as the first frost hit (and you should wait for that, to take the bitterness out), turnip greens, mustard greens, and collards were common fare—very common fare, maybe even everyday fare in the South. Turnip greens and black-eyed peas were on everyone's table, black or white, rich or poor, lunch or dinner.

For the queen, the simple combination of greens, black-eyed peas, rice and, if you had money, country ham was not only delicious, but it would bring great wealth and fabulous luck if eaten on New Year's Day. Why did hers taste so good and have such power? The secret, in part, was due to simple anticipation, the lengthy discussions, and the complicated gathering of ingredients.

The greens had to be fresh (in those days, your choices were fresh or canned, and canned greens at that time were horrific), so she spent a lot of time talking to friends, trying to find the best. In the post-war South, cans—replacing those Mason Jars, which had gone out of favor and were even declared illegal in certain sizes, as they made such great containers for moonshine—were the new-new thing. Frozen turnip greens were unheard of, so everything was canned, regardless of how awful it tasted, and that was very foolish, considering that most everything was actually very close at hand. The queen, however, knew fresh and would even ride to the farmers' market on Auburn Avenue if she could not find someone who would share from his garden or trade some fresh greens for the poke salad that sprang freely at her fence line.

She was careful with the amount of bacon fat and was very particular about the streak of lean (fat back). There had to be lots of black pepper and a fair amount of cayenne and Tabasco and salt. Anyway, who knew what everything really tasted like when we were so enraptured by the idea that all our wishes were coming true and all the money flowing in? So the dish, thanks to the queen's infusion of detail, captured everything wonderful about the South, about being a Georgian, about being close to the earth, even in winter, about remembering hard times, about savoring the present, about being fortified for good times and bad.

For some reason, you believed every word the queen said. And it was not just turnip greens and black-eyed peas she had you wishing on.

If you are the first to see that load of hay coming down the road, lick your thumb and stamp your hand, but never, never look back, or your wish will be annulled. And where on earth did she come up with the buzzard magic? "If a buzzard flaps his wings three times (trust me a rare event), make a wish fast, and it will be granted. Guaranteed." I cannot find the source of such nonsensical folklore in any literature. There was one sentence in *Miss Minerva and William Green Hill* about three buzzards. But still to this day, nothing keeps the duchess from stamping her hand on any load of hay and never looking back, even if she is driving and has to close her eyes to resist temptation. Just yesterday, gazing up into a sky emptied of everything but buzzards circling their prey, she was hoping for at least a single flap, the wish already loaded and ready.

Was it a spell the queen cast, or that she should have been a politician? Oh, that reminds me, her father was, among many other things, a politician; that is, the chairman of the Fulton County Commissioners in the '30s. He has no statue at the state capitol, but there are a few plaques on bridges inscribed with his name, Walter Ballard Stewart. And he did receive a letter from Bobby Jones, thanking him for the lovely parade the county had given in his honor. (The queen gave the letter to the Tiger-Eyed Princess's husband, Mr. Aristocrat.) While chairman, the queen's father also paved Northside Drive, the only straight road in Atlanta, which went, oddly enough, from the heart of Atlanta—Marietta

William Ballard Stewart

Street—right up to the Grant-Richardson (the most powerful family in Atlanta) property on Northside Drive. It is said that for this he received a new suit.

"A new suit for a fifteen-mile-long road. Is that not a stupid bribe to be proud of?" the queen would mutter.

Not to say she hadn't taken a Mason jar full of one-dollar bills from Mr. Aristocrat for the Bobby Jones autograph and the Calamity Jane putter that handsome Mr. Jones had given her. But who is to say whether she was telling the truth about the putter?

Place Is More Than A Setting

Over fifty years ago, almost sixty now, a boyfriend came to visit. Not just any boyfriend, but a handsome swimmer for the Canadian Olympic Team who loved to dance and party and chose, in an instant, someone who had rarely been chosen before, certainly not by a world-class athlete. He had transformed the duchess's college senior year into the frolic college should have been from the start. It was his first trip to the South, though he had heard of Sea Island, as had his fellow Canadians, and like other of his countrymen, he held no unexamined grudges against people from Georgia.

    The duchess and the swimmer were headed to a special place. The trip from Atlanta, Georgia, to Cashiers, North Carolina, was a little more difficult than usual as the recently widowed queen was bringing a load of her bird baths to sell in the hotel lobby. (She was oddly more interested in the painted patina of her creations than the present guest.) The car, while usually of sufficient size, did seem awkwardly crowded with the added bulk of the good-looking visitor, his knees hitting his chin as his foot room had been taken over by the garden ornaments. But this would doubtless be a perfect weekend. The duchess knew he would love the mountains, the hiking, the horse-back riding, the rustic, informal grandeur of High Hampton Inn.

    Things started going downhill almost immediately, as the boyfriend stepped out of the cramped car. His room was rather isolated from everyone else's and definitely too hot for his liking, lacking any air-conditioning. "Surely, you do not think that this is cool weather" were the first words he uttered.

    "Do not worry, we will be outside all the time, and tonight is Wednesday, which means roast beef and black-bottom pie."

    Unfortunately, the beef was well done with no other option presented, and he could not really enjoy the famous pie, as he was desperate for another scotch or even a beer. (Nothing alcoholic was served in the dining room, and the widowed queen had only brought vodka and was not sharing with much enthusiasm.)

"Why on earth," he muttered, "would one have to wear a tie to drink pre-sweetened tea with ice? I prefer my tea hot."

After a rather brief tour of the lake, which proved much too small by Canadian standards, and a shortened trail ride as all saddles were English, the duchess still remained optimistic as she had saved the best for last—the ritual hike up Chimney Top. As the swimmer was in excellent shape and in a hurry, the fun of anticipation and sense of accomplishment in attaining the summit were somewhat diminished. His only comment on the view at the top was "Gosh, you should see our Rockies. The sharp silhouettes reach to the skies, and the skiing there is awesome." And then he quickly turned to race back down and off.

It would be several more years before the duchess dared to return to this spot with someone for whom she might care. Again the arrival was testy. There was not a sign of blue sky as the three couples hopped out of the cars for the long weekend. The new suitor immediately hit his head on the low doorframe, but he only laughed, backed out, and then ceremoniously lowered his head for reentry. Pouring rain was the forecast every day. The rain, however, did not seem to bother the guys, so picking up a lone guest as their fourth, they set out for a round of golf. The story of that round of golf in torrential rain with the stranger, who shot a 61, carrying only three clubs, would be a story that lasted a lifetime for the duchess's date, as he pitted that one story against anyone's tale of witnessing a great moment in sports. The breakfast buffet of grits, eggs, bacon, country ham, and biscuits was, according to the date, the very best he had ever had, and he would make many pilgrimages throughout his life to recapture the rapture of that meal. Sitting around the blazing fire, commiserating with the other very sarcastic escorts, only seemed to intensify his delight in the place. Our duchess began to wonder if she should even suggest a hike with the weather still misty and dark clouds overhead. But her date was open to all adventures and was willing to try anything, the more daunting the better.

Only the two of them went. They had to proceed rather slowly as the rain had made the footing difficult, but even so, they were breathless as they reached the summit. Through the clouds, one could see for miles—the valley below, Georgia, and South Carolina in the distant, rounded mountains rolling into the beyond.

He asked, "Is that Whiteside over there?"

"Yes, you're right," replied the duchess.

"I have heard that Whiteside is the oldest mountain in the world. Do you think that De Soto really came this far inland? What is that mountain over there? Is there a bookshop nearby? We definitely need a map to identify so many peaks."

It would take a lifetime to name them all.

Samuel Boston Lathan (Dr. Prince's Grandfather)

It must be admitted that Dr. Prince's grandfather's fame as a soldier was due to a long life, his loquacious ways, and his skill as a scribbler rather than to his rank of private or the execution of countless notable deeds during the War of Northern Aggression. After all, he was barely twenty years old at the time of his service, and he was the one who had returned home to find that his dog had been shot. The grandfather's great moment was at South Mountain, the day before Bloody Antietam, when as he lay wounded, a passing Yankee tossed him a water-filled canteen, thus saving his life and giving him a true story to embellish and to confirm the romanticized Lost Cause saga. "Boss," as he was affectionately known, wisely managed to escape any future skirmishes or great battles by spending months either recuperating from his wound in a well-appointed Baltimore home or by walking, not riding, to his next duty post. All of Chester was spellbound with his storytelling and erudition (he read and taught both Greek and Latin), and the duchess often wished that she could've heard him describe the drink of water he received that fateful day.

And do not forget, Samuel Boston was the link to Dr. William Pressly, who introduced the duchess and Dr. Prince. Samuel Boston, Chester's most beloved academic, was the mentor that Bill Pressly, as a young scholar, had sought out and strove to imitate. What thin, precious threads weave us together, but for a drink on a battlefield or a well-conjugated verb.

The Duchess's Recipe from Charleston Receipts for Benne Seed Cookies

One of the few joint endeavors between the queen and her first-born daughter—inspired, of course, by the Tiger-Eyed Princess herself—was the discovery of the Benne Seed Cookies. One Christmas holiday, the Tiger-Eyed Princess returned from visiting a boyfriend, bringing benne seeds from Charleston and a Charleston Receipts cookbook. Somewhere the queen and the duchess had read that these seeds bring good luck. The queen knew only the tales of Ali Baba (Open, sesame!), but the duchess was sure she had read it from a transcribed oral history of a former slave. Whatever the case, they were both sure there was a well-proven theory that these seeds had special powers.

Using the Original Charleston Receipt (recipe), the queen and the duchess made cookies with these seeds—too late for Christmas but in time for New Year's. As many good things happened after that, Benne Seed Cookies became an added New Year's ritual. It may be that these cookies are just what cookies should be—simply great—but maybe they have more to them. Everybody wants these cookies on New Year's, and there is never a single one left by the end of the week. Dr. Prince always rambles around the kitchen, opening all the tins, pitifully searching for just one more. "Why only at New Year's?" he asks. He ought to know, since he was the one wished for and the one mysteriously conjured up.

¼ cup of butter
1 ½ cups of brown sugar
2 eggs
¼ teaspoon of baking powder
1 ¼ cups of flour
½ cup toasted benne seeds
1 teaspoon vanilla

Cream the butter and the sugar together. Add the other ingredients to the mixture in the order they are listed above. Line the bottom of a pan with waxed paper, and use a teaspoon to place the cookie dough on it. Leave room between the balls of dough; the cookies will spread as they bake.

Bake at 325 degrees, for 30 minutes. Makes 7 dozen.

Sarah Wilson's Spaghetti Sauce

There are some people whom you, the descendants, will never know, in spite of Karinthy's theory of six degrees of separation, Facebook, or Twitter. These people are simply gone from life, vanished into the past, they have been forgotten—even tossed—though they may have been the godmother, the closest neighbor, a dearest friend. One such person was Sarah Wilson. During the early years of World War II and in the years immediately following the war, most all of the just-marrieds lived in apartments, and the Wilsons lived in an apartment complex across from 2788 Peachtree Road. The queen loved the Wilsons, for she could often send her little princess over to their apartment for a welcomed break. The king did not want his daughter shuffled off, and he imagined numerous dangers in the queen's practice. But even though she knew her father didn't approve, the young princess looked forward to spending the night with the Wilsons, especially on Thursdays when Sarah made her spaghetti.

    This sauce remains a staple in the life of the duchess, and when she makes it, she sometimes remembers Sarah for a moment. Nonetheless, the king was prescient in that this dish (and thus, by extension, the Wilsons themselves) would prove to be subversive. The sauce's wonderful taste relied heavily on canned, easy-to-find, and inexpensive ingredients, thus wrecking Southern cuisine for decades. Everyone jumped on the canned-and-easy revolution, erroneously assuming that everything canned and easy tasted good. No doubt, the ease of this recipe was also a major factor in keeping women in the workforce and liberated after the war had ended and the men came home. What husband could complain that his wife was gone all day when he was served such delicious fare?

    This recipe is a door to freedom if you make it early in the morning. Cook it while you get breakfast and everyone out of the house. It can then just sit until you finally return home and put it back on the stove for more simmering; this is, of course, its secret. The sauce is even better the next day.

> Brown some ground beef (just a patty is enough) in a large iron skillet.
>
> Saute a chopped Spanish onion and a few stalks of celery in olive oil.

Add:
> One large jar of prepared spaghetti sauce
> (Prego works fine)
> A couple of cans of stewed tomatoes
> A lot of oregano
> Salt and pepper
> 1 tablespoon of vinegar (the duchess adds several of balsamic vinegar to the browning beef)

As always, the queen added tabasco and 1/2 teaspoon of red pepper.

About an hour before you serve the meal, add chopped green pepper and a bay leaf; add more water if needed.

 Sister—Kathleen Hudson Garner

While some friends disappear forever, with no strings attached, relatives are permanently connected, even though they too have dissolved into specters, shadowed and remote. One might have been baptized with their name or have found it listed in a will, but no one remembers these relatives now, and only the genealogists remain interested.

Yet, if only in a fragment, Sister must be included in the tale of the duchess. Just because.

Sister was the oldest of the king's four siblings. As we know, their father was a Methodist minister. Still, growing up in the very fragile world of turn-of-the-nineteenth-century Georgia, Sister was the only one of the four children who kept the strong commitment to the family's faith. Also, in spite of the king's Phi Beta Kappa key, Sister was the closest to being brilliant. She completed college at a time when few women—and especially few Southern women—did. She is the one who translated Latin assignments for the king when he was tutoring the rich in New York City. He would mail the assignments home, and she would make the corrections and translations and mail the scholar's work back, just so her brother could shine as a tutor extraordinaire.

She married properly (except that her husband, Ross Garner, was a Baptist); he worked for Southern Bell. They had no children. And though she lived in a two-bedroom apartment, it was Sister who took the king's mother in. The queen had gone berserk when the king brought his mother to live with them in the not-too-small house.

Sister was very thin, small, and attractive. She was bright, active in the church, and thrifty. Because she dutifully cooked according to a strict diabetic diet (her husband required it), Sister lived to almost one hundred years of age. However, it was from Sister that the duchess learned one could eat chocolate and still be thin. Sister would often go to her stash, hidden so as not to tempt, smiling and saying, "Just one after dinner for just you and me will not hurt a thing."

The king honored his sister by giving the Tiger-Eyed Princess her name, but it was the discarded princess he took on all his visits to Sister's home. The discarded princess in turn tried to connect with this very fine and competent woman, taking her own children to visit on Christmas Eve, cheering with her Neil Armstrong's incredible walk on the moon, joining both Garners for dinner at Mary Mac's; but in her so, so busy world, our princess failed to hold on tight enough to this self-sufficient saint.

Sister did leave the discarded princess, in addition to a large manila envelope with many newspaper clippings celebrating the princess's accomplishments, a larger portion (not really very much more) of her estate than either of her two siblings, although she gave most of it to another nephew who had taken over her care. The discarded princess took the money and immediately installed a sprinkler system in her backyard, saying in a little prayer, "Thank you, thank you, Sister. A little extravagance is a wonderful thing."

Now that the family has moved from the yellow house and the descendants cannot see Sister's sprinklers joyfully playing and the hydrangeas so blue in the water's spray, only one thing from Sister lives on: a recipe from Macon. (Surely, you cannot count Measured Rice Krispies with Skim Milk a recipe worth saving, though it was a breakfast that brought Sister long life, and it might do the same for you. In any case, here is her torte.)

Len Berg's Saltine-Date Torte

(Len Berg's was a popular lunch spot in Macon, Georgia.)

> 12 saltines, crushed
> 12 dates, cut-up
> ½ cup chopped pecans
> ¾ cup sugar
> ½ teaspoon baking powder
> 3 egg whites
> 1 teaspoon vanilla
> 1 teaspoon water

Beat egg whites, the vanilla, and the water together. Combine the first four ingredients, then fold the first mixture into the second one. Bake about 30 minutes at 350 degrees. Serve with whipped cream. Do not be fooled by the recipe's simplicity. It is really quite elegant. Is there a lesson in her deliberate, simple life as well?

Where do you think her silver bangle bracelets are? I can hear them jingling now as she moves briskly around her apartment to reach for the still hidden, though Ross is gone, box of chocolates to share with you.

Beware

The queen was a great storyteller and loved to gather her children around her in her large canopied bed. After she had tired of reading and reading, she would tell wonderful tales about growing up in Georgia. Her father, Walter Stewart, was from a fine Middle Georgia family, the Woolfolks. He was quite handsome, and sometimes even rich, but absent most of the time, making money or losing it and who knows what else. Her mother, Louise Clark Stewart, was also well connected to the Georgia gentry from Sumter County and stayed at home, but she wasn't really present, as she could not stop grieving for a son who had died as a baby.

With no real parental oversight, the queen, as a child, was free to roam wherever, get into as much trouble as she could, taunt or be taunted by her older brother, or play mother to her younger brother, but only if she felt like it. The three children had a goat cart to ride, chicken coops in which to hide, guinea hens to chase, red clay dust to wash constantly off their bare feet, and there was always laughter coming from the kitchen, where the farm help gathered for breakfast and lunch. A life completely undisciplined was her sunshine in which to bask. She was smart enough to enjoy every minute of it: squashing muscadines with her toes, following Man Pitt around as he gathered in the wood, eating only when she was ready (which usually meant joining the farm help at the kitchen table after the adults had finished and gone up for a nap), even playing with the doodlebug holes in the sand underneath the porch as afternoon lingered and turned to twilight—everything at once innocent and of little consequence.

The queen's children loved these stories about her carefree childhood and begged to hear them over and over, but when they grew older and pressed for more details—"Where is your plantation now? Who are these Woolfolks, Canteys, and Clarks? Wasn't anyone ever famous?"—she would suddenly stop the storytelling, ignore the pleading for more, and get up. All questions were dismissed as foolish. The off button, with no explanation, had been pushed.

While the Woolfolks were one of the most outstanding families in the Stewart's family tree (there were stories aplenty, I am sure, to tell of American Revolution-era militia men, of Georgia's first female doctor, of pre- and post-Civil War planters), all stories about these prominent forbearers seemed to disappear. The Benjamin Stewarts became a family without a past at all, as far as the queen's family was concerned. Walter Stewart, the queen's father, did join the Robert Burns Society, embracing a more distant Scottish past—a chorus or two of "Auld Lang Syne" was sufficient remembering for him. Louise Clark Stewart, the queen's mother, hid herself writing gentle nature poems (I am still searching for copies), waxing on about dogwoods and crepe myrtles. Once their children were grown, Louise and Walter were divorced, and Louise moved to Washington, D.C., to become an anonymous government employee. She remained too shaken by the tragic loss of her first born and the shenanigans of her husband to worry about the heroics or horrors that belonged to those who had come before.

The queen relished this "pastlessness," this unusual Southern silence. She knew she could manage by her wits alone. Had she not entertained herself all through her youth? She needed no lineage to pull her through: she had no fears; she felt no guilt. She could invent whatever was needed. Luck would be the queen's lady, and she was ready with daring to play any hand she was dealt.

What had happened so long ago? Why did the queen become so remote when asked for more stories? Did justice, injustice, pure terror, or prolonged innocence prevail? Isn't understanding of our forbearers necessary if we are to ever get it right ourselves, apply the most soothing balm, dispel the lingering sadness? Is the past to be left in silence and intact like some chain of linked remorse that will never break, leaving a sense that there will always be unidentifiable loss to which we are all bound and are held accountable?

Or is our gift from the queen the insight that longing—which seems to spring from our family's past—is really just the wish to once again join the warm circle of laughter, after all who would pass judgment have left, around the kitchen table in the back? Are the stories, not the truth, all we really want or need?

Or is there something more?

 Samuel Whigham – The Last Dance

Often the most unbelievable part of a story is that which comes closest to the truth. The queen never doubted that a handsome, rich, fun, extraordinary man would suddenly appear in her life and redeem, through his absolute devotion to her, the many, many years of unhappiness and loneliness she had spent as a child, a mother, a wife, and a widow. She never dreamed, however, that it would take so long.

In fact, it was twenty years, give or take a few, after the death of the king, before the queen received a call from Sam—Sir Sam, to be more accurate. Sir Sam and the queen had both grown up in Hapeville, and while they had dated and Sir Sam had obviously remembered, their lives took very different paths and had never recrossed. Sir Sam had been happily married. He was the retired treasurer of Grady Hospital and had no children. His wife had just died. He was calling to take the queen out.

Now the queen at this time, after waiting—not really very patiently but still hoping for her prince charming—had not, at least to anyone's knowledge, given Sir Sam a second thought. In fact, at the very moment when he called, the first possible prospect ever in twenty years (actually a king, besides) had appeared. The queen said "yes" to Sir Sam more to stir up her new suitor than to reconnect with her Hapeville past. Sir Sam had his work cut out for him, and the family all waited, holding their breath. Did Sir Sam have any idea what he was getting into? After all, he was not particularly tall, not fabulously wealthy, nor overly sophisticated. His main redeeming attribute, at first, was that he was a graduate of Georgia Tech. And he was extraordinary in his pursuit.

The whole family, including Mattie (it was just learned), saw Sir Sam as the queen's best choice. The duchess, as the oldest, assumed the worry mantle, as she was the one who had to witness (as did her running companions on their early morning jogs) the different cars parked outside the queen's house ... one morning a gray one, the next day the black.

One will never know whose prayers were answered, but the queen, at age sixty-nine, and Sir Sam were married on the big porch of 19 Brookhaven Drive in a lovely ceremony. The bride wore fuschia, the color in which she looked best, and was quite giddy, while Sir Sam's smile was almost heart breaking. Their life together was as wonderful as the queen had imagined it. Sir Sam loved her with all his heart.

And what adventures they had. There was the trip to Mexico City, during which they, now both in their eighties, drove the black Mercedes the whole distance from Atlanta rather than fly, because the queen wanted to stop by Avery Island on the way down to visit the home of Tabasco, her favorite ingredient of all time, and on the return to take golf lessons in Texas from Walter Penick, the best golf coach in the world. No one believed they would come back alive. The Mercedes would, at the very least, be lost as ransom.

And there was Pat's funeral service.

The queen had always longed for a staff, the staff she had left somewhere behind when she married the king, the proper and complete staff she envisioned. Mattie had been but one person and besides had retired some time ago. In these years, Sir Sam did so much of the work. He organized the queen's finances, paid all the bills, got the right insurance, washed his own dishes, always opened the door, and remembered and held the umbrella. One could not imagine anything else he might do, and besides, he was so sweet and so kind to her, laughing at her whims, happy to be on such a rollercoaster. Still, the queen wanted a staff, often talked about this, and was always on the lookout. By chance she learned that the Throwers' fine housekeeper did have an extra day, and Margaret Thrower assured her that Pat was excellent. She made delicious chicken salad and served beautifully; her uncle had been

Julius, the head maitre d' at the Piedmont Driving Club in the '40s and '50s. Pat's credentials were impeccable, and the queen wondered if she would qualify in Pat's eyes.

Pat did prove to be excellent. She was willing to do any task, immediately caught on to the dream they were attempting to live, and spontaneously added a few flourishes of her own in terms of service and decorum. She helped the queen dress, just as the queen had so often yearned, adjusting her lingerie, fastening her bra, folding her skirt as she stepped out of it for a quick nap.

Old age was not stopping the Whighams, but after only a few months, Pat started complaining about not feeling well. The queen was concerned and called Dr. Prince. He assured her that if the symptoms persisted, she should send Pat in and he would be happy to see her.

"Perhaps it's just menopause—the tiredness, shortness of breath, the sudden hot flashes," the queen suggested.

"Those problems could easily be addressed," responded Dr. Prince.

Pat never went to see the doctor, and only a few months after the queen's call, the queen announced that Pat had suddenly died.

There was much discussion about the funeral. Was it proper to go, knowing her for only a relatively short time? Would they get lost trying to find their way to the other side of town? But Sam was always willing to drive, the Throwers said they were going, and they all had directions to the church.

It was late in the afternoon when the queen called, her voice trembling. She could hardly speak. "There has been, there has been a sort, a sort of tragedy," she finally said.

"Is Sir Sam all right? Are you okay."

"We are all in shock. I cannot breathe."

What had happened? The duchess suddenly was worried about the queen, for this was the first time in her life she had ever heard her mother actually shaken, undone.

The queen tried to get it out. She began by saying, "We had to stop at the Varsity, the Throwers and Sir Sam and I, for a Coke-Cola, just to collect ourselves. None of us could drive home in the state we were in. It is all so unimaginable."

After much back and forth, this is the story that emerged:

The queen and Sir Sam found the church with little effort and were ushered into the vestibule to see that the church was filled. They were asked if they wished to view the body and, not wanting to appear rude, agreed to walk the long aisle to pay their last respects at the casket. When they looked down, they saw that a man lay there, dressed in a rather fine suit and tie. The queen nudged Sam and whispered, "You've brought me to the wrong church. We need to a leave. And now." As they turned to exit quickly and find the right funeral, they noticed that the Throwers also were in the wrong place, as were several of their friends. Obviously, all of them had the same incorrect directions and had not looked into the casket, for they were still sitting quietly in their pews. The queen and Sir Sam walked briskly by, attempting unobtrusive hand signals to the Throwers, Sam barely hanging on, and politely nodded to the usher saying that they needed to leave to attend another funeral. "What funeral are you attending?" he asked. When Sir Sam responded, the usher replied, "But this is Pete's funeral."

"Pete's funeral? We're going to Pat's."

"Yes, this is Pat's funeral." Then he softly added, "His mother is, of course, distraught by his death, but rejoices that she finally has her son back."

"His mother may have her son back, but I've just lost every shred of human dignity I ever had," the queen thought.

The queen and Sir Sam then turned slowly back around, faced the altar, and took their seats, breathless and still shaking, to hear about the wonders of God's mercy, the power and glory of the resurrection.

There was even more humiliation as the queen and Sir Sam soon learned that all the Park Place staff, from the concierge to the valet parking crew, knew that Pat was Pete, or Pete was Pat, and all had enjoyed, as Pat-Pete must have, the wonderful charade that was transpiring every week. I hope Pat-Pete did enjoy his role, for he was a star. Perhaps your best role is always to play your real self regardless of what your mother might want. And it probably hurts no one, not even you, to play the role your mother wished for with that very last breath you have. Few, however, are lucky enough to swing both before that great sweet chariot descends to carry them home.

I think it wonderful and well deserved that it was Sir Sam who got to witness and share the queen being fooled by her own foolish dreams. Their life together was a dance for sure and perhaps the best dance of all, as it was the last.

The Iron Skillet

Everything is so different now. For those of us born in the '40s, our heroic attempts at being modern are like the word "modern" itself, just a signifier of a period in history, the details of which are beloved by film directors and collectors, irrelevant to the imperial present. The infinity we sought and revolutions we fought are merely a series of brackets—[circa 1930–1950]. New injustices will be discovered, some actually rectified, and even in a democracy, amendments added. But you can be sure that it will be mercy, not justice, you will want the most; it will be mercy, not justice, you will wish you had given; and it is you who must let the stranger in, that is if you wish to dance.

Oh, well, there is one object you will need from the past, if not to cook with, at least for your museum. The iron skillet was always present in your family history, backstage or in the spotlight, and in spite of hilarious laughter or great suffering, globalization, fast food, the iPhone, or whatever your most proud possession may become, I suggest you hang on to at least one of the iron skillets you might find in the kitchen cabinets when you start throwing everything out. It is definitely too heavy to carry around in your backpack, so you will also need a place to put it.

This was going to be a discussion on seasoning the iron skillet (for the seasoning is its secret), but there are detailed instructions on the Internet. Just in case the Internet, like all our 45 rpm records, disappears from the face of the earth, remember to rinse the skillet out by hand, not putting it in the dishwasher, and if rust does peek through, give your skillet a good rubbing of lard, bacon grease, oil, or whatever fat they haven't outlawed, and heat it up in the oven at around 200 degrees for a couple of hours. Let it sit till it cools, and then wipe any remaining oil off with a paper towel. Use it often, for it improves with wear.

The iron skillet, like fire itself, will be an eternal component of any great home cooked meal. At least this I believe.

The beginning and ending..are they ever the same?

Sincerely, your Duchess.

www.ingramcontent.com/pod-product-compliance
Lightning Source LLC
Chambersburg PA
CBHW042307150426
43197CB00005B/100